LIFE-TIME SPORTS FOR THE COLLEGE STUDENT

Contributing Authors

Betty Jean Duffy
Bucks County Community College

Joan Ferry
Pennridge Public Schools

Wayne Hughes
Bucks County Community College

John Kuchinsky
Bucks County Community College

Barbara Leighton
West Chester State College

Wesley Olsen
Ogontz Campus, The Pennsylvania State University

Andrew C. Ostrow
University of California, At Berkeley

Eugene Schaefer
Bucks County Community College

Marcia Trinkley
Bucks County Community College

Martin Zwiren
University of Bridgeport

LIFE-TIME SPORTS FOR THE COLLEGE STUDENT

A BEHAVIORAL OBJECTIVE APPROACH

Eugene R. Fox, Ed.D.
Barry L. Sysler

Bucks County Community College
Newtown, Pennsylvania

KENDALL/HUNT PUBLISHING COMPANY
DUBUQUE, IOWA

Contents

Preface

This textbook is directed to the male and female college students who will be living in a society which is becoming increasingly complicated. In order to live effectively in this society, physical and mental well-being is imperative.

It is our belief that the physical and mental well-being of students can be enhanced by a college physical education program which is designed to teach, *Life-Time Sports*. Life-time sports are activities in which the student can participate throughout most of his life span. All the activities in this text are considered to be life-time sports.

It is imperative for the student to have an opportunity to select the specific activities in which he is interested. In order to meet our objectives of good physical and mental well-being through participation in life-time sports, the student must be truely interested in the specific activity and he must achieve success.

The educational process is concerned with changing the behavior of the learner so that he is able to display a behavior which he did not previously exhibit. Behavioral objectives are expectations or outcomes that guide the learner during the period of instruction. They specify what the learner must be able to do or perform when he is demonstrating his mastery of the objective. Thus, a behavioral objective is one that identifies the kind of performance that will be accepted as evidence that the learner has successfully achieved the stated objective. A precise statement of objectives enables the learner to know exactly what is expected of him, under what conditions, and what standards of performance if any. The student is then provided with a means of evaluating his own progress at any given time during the instructional period.

With a clear understanding of these goals, the learner eventually becomes aware of those specific skills which are relevant to his success. The mutual understanding of goals between learner and teacher greatly facilitates instruction; knowledge of what the learner is striving to achieve serves to more effectively motivate a student to achieve that end.

Each of the following chapters includes a section listing the behavioral objectives of that particular life-time activity. It should be noted that the essential criteria for each skill have been incorporated into the context of the respective chapters. In addition, the text has been designed so that the degree of proficiency necessary to achieve each of the behavioral objectives will be demonstrated when the learner can consistently perform each of the basic skills (successfully demonstrate each skill in two out of three attempts). No attempt has been made to include all the objectives necessary to develop an extremely high level of skill. Rather, it is the hope of the authors that those objectives listed will guide the learner in developing a level of skill which will enable him to successfully perform in each of these sports, while enjoying such activities throughout his life.

The book includes a comprehensive analysis of each activity and a thorough explanation and discussion of every phase of the activities. Each chapter is devoted to one sport and consists of behavioral objectives, history, nature of the sport, equipment, skills to be developed, terminology, rules, and a bibliography.

The contributing authors have added an extraordinary amount of expertise in their specific disciplines. These writers were selected because of their knowledge and experience in teaching their respective skills to college students. The authors are also indebted to Mr. Bernard Forer, who constructively evaluated the manuscript.

ARCHERY

BEHAVIORAL OBJECTIVES

1. Given the tackle, the college student will be able to successfully demonstrate (meet *all* of the essential criteria as specified in the chapter) the following basic techniques of target shooting:
   a. Stance.
   b. Nocking the arrow.
   c. Drawing the bow.
   d. Anchoring.
   e. Aiming.
   f. Releasing.
   g. Follow-through.
2. The college student will be able to achieve a score of at least 75 per cent on a written examination concerned with the history, safety rules, proper selection and care of equipment, terminology and analysis of archery fundamentals.

HISTORY OF ARCHERY

The actual time and place of origin of archery is unknown, but it can be traced back to the caveman. The first bow was used as a weapon of survival and established man's superiority over animals. Hand-to-hand combat with his enemies was no longer necessary. The bow and arrow meant food, clothing and protection.

The bow and arrow were used on all continents except Australia, and can be seen entwined in man's culture. Enthralled with the hum of the bowstring, additional strings were added to form *David's Harp*. Individuals associated with archery in Greek mythology include: *Apollo*, god of archery; *Eros* or *Cupid*, symbol of love; *Diana*, goddess of wild things; the *Amazons*, female Greek warriors; and *Achilles*, a Greek warrior who was hit in the heel with a poisoned arrow. Today anatomists call that area the *Achilles tendon*.

The English developed their famous longbow, noting that increased bow length meant increased range. England was also the first country to shoot from horseback, which increased shooting range. The French developed the crossbow, which was originally designed by the Orientals. The longbow meant superior rapid shooting and distance, but the crossbow developed superior accuracy and power. (See Figure 1-1)

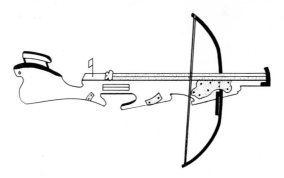

Figure 1-1. The Crossbow.

In 1828, competitive archery was introduced to the United States with the formation of the United Bowmen of Philadelphia Club. This group is still in existence today and shoots on a regular basis. The National Archery Association (N.A.A.) was organized in 1879. (See Figure 1-2) The N.A.A. sponsors a National Tournament each year and serves to perpetuate the ancient sport. The N.A.A., along with many other countries, joined to form the Internationale de Tir a la' Arc, commonly called F.I.T.A. Tournaments are held every two years in various countries. The first in the United States

Figure 1-2. Archery Insignias: F.I.T.A., N.A.A. and N.F.A.A.

occurred at Valley Forge Park in 1969. A more recent organization, formed to give hunters practice, is the National Field Archery Association. The first competition for this group took place in 1946. Archery has recently been reinstated as an official Olympic sport beginning with the 1972 games.

The uses of archery today are quite varied. Most participants take part in recreational target archery, field archery, and bow hunting, while others try their hand at fishing with the bow and arrow. Naturalists use a hypodermic needle propelled with a bow to drug animals. This method is used to acquire animals for zoological gardens and to restock game areas. The art of silent killing is taught to a limited few in the Armed Forces today. With the introduction of indoor archery lanes, archery has become a year round sport, which enables bowmen to practice and compete during inclement weather.

NATURE OF ARCHERY

Archery is primarily a sport of shooting arrows at a target. The sport appeals to both sexes, all ages, and is considered a lifetime activity. Target archery has an appeal to the handicapped, while field archery and hunting offer a challenge to the most rigorous individual. Basic shooting skills developed in target archery may subsequently be used in such novelty events as flight shooting, clout shooting, and bow fishing.

Target Archery

The archer shoots a definite number of arrows from specified distances at a target face composed of five or ten circles. (See Figure 1-3)

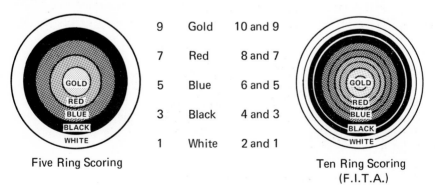

9	Gold	10 and 9
7	Red	8 and 7
5	Blue	6 and 5
3	Black	4 and 3
1	White	2 and 1

Five Ring Scoring

Ten Ring Scoring
(F.I.T.A.)

Figure 1-3. Five and Ten Ring Scoring.

Field Archery

Field archery is competition in which archers shoot at 28 stationary targets of assorted sizes at different, but standardized distances. Field archery is excellent practice for the hunter and is analogous to a golfer moving from hole to hole on a golf course. (See Figure 1-4)

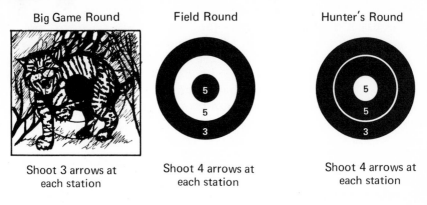

Figure 1-4. Field Archery Target Faces.

In the big game round, a hit with any arrow terminates the shooting at that target. Scoring values follow:

1st arrow: 20 points for vital organ, 15 for rest of animal.

2nd arrow: 15 points for vital organ, 10 for rest of animal.

3rd arrow: 10 points for vital organ, 5 for rest of animal.

The field and hunter's round are quite similar to each other. Target size and scoring are the same. Distances shot are greater in the field round than the hunter and they are posted, but distances are not marked for the hunter's round.

Flight Shooting

In flight shooting, arrows are shot for maximum distance. Special flight arrows are used, and competition is held in regular or free-style classes. A normal bow is used in the regular class, while a footed bow is used in the free-style class. In *pedominal* shooting the archer lies on his back, holds the bow with his feet and pulls the string with his hands to achieve distances beyond 700 yards. (See Figure 1-5)

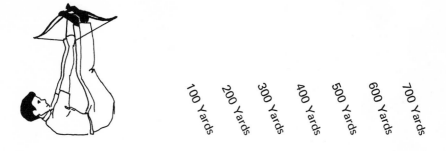

Figure 1-5. Flight Shooting.

Clout Shooting

Clout shooting is a competitive round in which thirty-six arrows are shot at a ground target forty-eight feet in diameter. The center is marked with a white flag, while the target is marked with a chain painted in the same colors as a standard target face. Scoring values are similar. The range for women is 120 or 140 yards, while the men's range is 180 yards.

To retrieve and score arrows, one archer stands behind each color as the chain is rotated in a circle. (See Figure 1-6) Archers pull arrows in their colored area of the chain as it is rotated and then place all arrows in that colored area for scoring. (See Figure 1-7) Each shooter walks the length of the chain and scores his arrows.

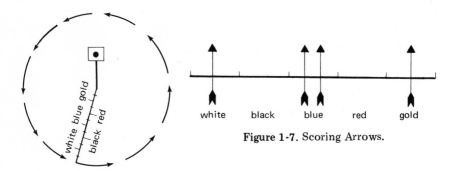

Figure 1-7. Scoring Arrows.

Figure 1-6. Rotating Chain.

EQUIPMENT (TACKLE)

Bows

Bows can be constructed in two ways. The *self* bow is made from one type of material. The *laminated* or *composition* bow is made of various materials, such as wood or plastic, and the layers are glued together. The novice should select a light bow and gradually work into using a heavier bow. A fiberglass bow is excellent for beginners. It may be straight or recurved. (See Figure 1-8) The *straight* bow is straight when unstrung, the *recurved* bow has ends which curve toward the back to permit the bow to shoot faster and further than the straight bow. Some bows have a center shot or area above the handle cut out to allow a clear view of the target and to permit straight string pressure. (See Figure 1-9) Experienced archers may use a laminated recurve center shot fiberglass bow with a hardwood core.

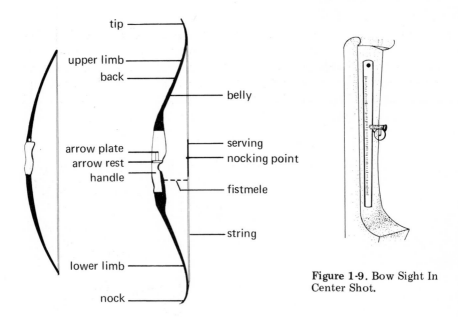

tip

upper limb

back

belly

arrow plate

arrow rest

handle

serving

nocking point

fistmele

string

lower limb

nock

Figure 1-9. Bow Sight In Center Shot.

Figure 1-8. Straight Bow and Recurved Bow.

Bow weights are determined by the number of pounds required to draw the string a specified distance. Most bows are marked for the bow weight of a twenty-eight inch draw and can be found on the lower bow limb below the handle. For each inch over or under the twenty-eight inch draw, the weight increases or decreases approximately two pounds. Women generally prefer bows pulling 20-30 pounds, men usually select a bow in the 30-40 pound range.

Length is a second consideration when selecting a bow. Bows range from fifty-two to seventy-two inches. Longer bows are becoming more popular because the draw is easier, a factor to be considered in tournament shooting. The weight of the bow is also increased which results in steadying the hand of the archer. Suggested bow lengths to match arrow lengths for beginners are listed below.

Arrow Length	Bow Length
24″ to 25″	5′0″ to 5′3″
26″ to 27″	5′4″ to 5′6″
28″ to 30″	5′7″ to 5′10″

Arrows

Arrows are the most important part of the archer's tackle. (See Figure 1-10) The correct length is found by placing the nock end against the breastbone, bringing the hands forward on either side, palms facing so the fingertips reach the near end of the arrow tip. (See Figure 1-11) It is safer to select a long arrow rather than a short

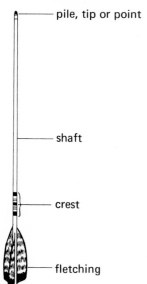

pile, tip or point

shaft

crest

fletching

nock

Figure 1-10. Parts of an Arrow.

Figure 1-11. Selecting Arrow Length.

arrow. Overdrawing a short arrow could result in injury to the archer's hand. Arrow lengths for women commonly range from 23 to 28 inches, while the range for men is 25 to 30 inches.

The second item to consider in arrow selection is *spine*, a combination of stiffness and flexibility in the shaft of an arrow. When selecting the proper spine, consider arrow length and weight, the type of arrow point, and the bow weight (pounds of pull exerted on the bow string for your specific arrow length).

As the arrow leaves the bow it appears to fly straight to the target. For a right-handed archer, the arrow goes to the left when it leaves the bow, stabilizes itself in flight and then travels to the target. This is known as the *Archer's Paradox*. Too much spine or stiffness in an arrow will cause the shaft to overbend and send the arrow to the right of the target. If the spine is too weak or flexible, the arrow will never stabilize and always fly to the left of the target. Devices to measure spine and charts are available in matching arrows to your bow.

Arrows may also vary in diameter, with the wider ones being stronger. Arrows should be selected and marked for the bow weight with which they may be used. This weight should equal or be greater than the weight of the bow. The arrow shaft will be able to absorb the pounds of pressure sent through it. If the arrow is less than the marked bow weight, the arrow could splinter.

When selecting arrows, look for matched arrows. They should be similar in spine (amount of stiffness), weight, color and size of feathers, length and crest. Wooden arrows, generally made of Port Orford cedar, are the least expensive. They may warp, but may be straightened by holding over heated water and bending back in position. Wooden arrows may be self arrows (a single piece of wood) or footed arrows (hardwood spliced into the foreshaft for more strength, weight, and better balance). Fiberglass arrows are quite reasonably priced and have the advantage of not warping. The best arrows made today are aluminum and are favored by advanced archers.

Arrow points or *piles* vary according to use. They include: target piles, broadheads or hunting tips, fishing barbs, and blunt tips. (See Figure 1-12) The *fletching* or feathers are larger on hunting arrows than on target arrows. *Flu-flus* or spiral shaped feathers decrease distance and are used in novelty events. Bow fishing feathers are made of plastic, rubber or other material suitable for water. (See Figure 1-13)

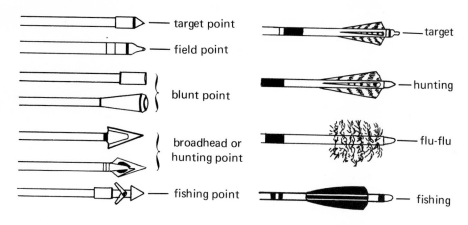

Figure 1-12. Types of Arrow Tips.   Figure 1-13. Types of Fletchings.

Bowstrings

Bow length and weight must always be considered when selecting a bowstring. The most satisfactory strings are made of Dacron or Fortisan, and may be single or double looped. Double looped strings permit little adjustment. A timber hitch knot is used to secure a single looped string to the lower bow nock. (See Figure 1-14) Frayed strings should be replaced immediately. Strings should be waxed with beeswax, except the serving which may take a coating of celluloid cement or paraffin. A nocking point on the bowstring is helpful in improving accuracy, since the arrow is released from the same spot each time. The mark on the serving may be a knot, thread, ink, or small metal ring and should be below the arrow when it is placed in the bowstring. The string should be a *fistmele*, approximately six inches, from the belly of the bow.

Finger Tabs or Shooting Gloves

A finger tab, a flat piece of leather which goes between the three shooting fingers and string, or shooting glove should be worn for protection and for a smooth release. (See Figure 1-15) Cordovan finger tabs are interchangeable, inexpensive, and protect against blisters. Hold the tab in the left hand with the shiny side up and holes to the right. Put the first and third fingers of the right hand through the holes to expose fingertips as the tab is pressed back against the fingers. Be sure the tab is between the shooting fingers and string.

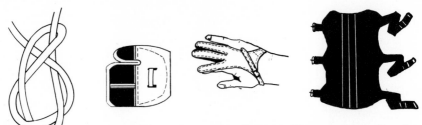

Figure 1-15. Finger Tab, Shooting Glove, and Arm Guard.

Figure 1-14.
Timber Hitch
Knot.

The shooting glove offers more protection, but must be selected for individual size. Place the middle three fingers into the glove with the leather back against the back of the hand and adjust the strap buckle.

Arm Guards

An arm guard should be worn on the inner forearm of the extended arm to prevent string slap, and to hold long-sleeved clothing close to the arm. To secure, buckle or lace the guard on the back of the forearm. (See Figure 1-15)

Quivers

Quivers may be stationary or movable. Metal ground quivers have a pointed tip at the bottom and are circular or rectangular at the top. Arrows are held in the circle, and some quivers have supports for a bow. Field archers prefer hip, shoulder, or pocket quivers. (See Figure 1-16)

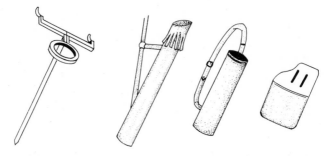

Figure 1-16. Ground, Hip, Shoulder, and Pocket Quivers.

Targets and Stands

Bales of straw set one on top of another are economical. Upper and lower bales should be rotated into the center position to prolong their use. Cover the top bale with plastic to protect from the rain. Portable targets consist of straw wound in a circle. The standard size is 48-inches in diameter. Portable targets should be stored flat and carried, never rolled, to target stands. New lightweight excelsior and plastic foam targets are now available for indoor and outdoor use.

Stands may be soft white pine tripods or movable carriers secured to the ground with a wire or rope to prevent them from blowing over. Place the target in an unobstructed open area with sufficient distance (at least 30 feet) behind for retrieving arrows. A hill in back of the target makes arrow retrieving easier.

Target Faces

The circular target face is made of oil cloth, painted in nonglare colors consisting of a gold center 9 3/5 inches in diameter and four concentric rings each 4 3/5 inches in width colored red, light blue, black, and white. The edge beyond the white ring *(petticoat)* should be 1 inch wide. The target face is skirted and is attached to the target with a draw string. The standard size is 48-inches in diameter. The center of the gold area should be four feet from the ground and the target should be tilted slightly skyward. Squared paper target faces should have a cardboard backing before being attached to the target with wire target pins.

SKILLS TO BE DEVELOPED

Shooting Right- or Left-Handed

Your dominant eye should determine which way you shoot. Face an object, such as the target, extend both arms, palms open toward the object. Overlap the two hands and thumbs so there is a small opening between the two hands. With both eyes open, center the object in the opening made by the hands. Close the left eye; if the object remains in the opening, you have a dominant right eye and should shoot right-handed (holding the bow in your left hand). If the object moved, your left eye is dominant, so shoot left-handed. If the left eye is dominant, but you prefer to shoot right-handed, you must close the left eye while aiming or there will be a tendency to shoot to the left. When judging distance shoot with both eyes open, but be sure the shooting or trigger arm is on the dominant eye side. If "nondominance" is found, shoot from the most natural side.

Instructions are orientated to right-handed application, reverse if left-handed.

Bracing the Bow

Two ways of stringing the bow are the *pull-push method*, used for light or straight bows, and the *step-through method*, used for heavy or recurved bows. (See Figure 1-17 and Figure 1-18) The bowstring loops should be on the limbs before the bow is braced. The top bowstring loop slips over and down the upper limb to permit the loop to go into the lower limb nock.

Figure 1-17. Push-Pull Method of Bracing the Bow.

Figure 1-18. Step-Through Method of Bracing the Bow.

Pull-Push Method

1. Place the tip of the lower limb against the left instep. Be sure the bow does not touch the ground.
2. With the back of the bow facing the body, simultaneously pull the handle with the left hand and push the upper limb down with the heel of the right hand.
3. While maintaining this pressure, the right thumb and forefinger slide up the bow and slip the loop into the nock.
4. Before removing the pressure, check to see that the upper loop is completely in the upper nock.

To unbrace the bow, use the same body position. Pull with the left hand and push down with the heel of the right hand to loosen the string. Maintain this position and lift the string from the nock with the index and middle fingers of the right hand. Let the string down, not off, the upper limb. Keep fingers on the outside of the bow to prevent pinching them between the string and bow.

Step-Through Method
1. Place the lower loop of the bowstring in the lower nock.
2. Hold the bow upright and rest the lower end of the bow on the instep of the left foot so the limb is flat.
3. With the belly of the bow facing forward, step between the string and bow with the right leg.
4. Bring the inside of the handle against the back of the right thigh.
5. Push forward with the right hand on the upper limb and use the left hand to guide the string into place. Avoid twisting the lower limb.
6. Be sure the string is secure in both nocks before releasing bow pressure.

To unbrace the bow, reverse the above procedure. Always unstring the bow after using and hang vertically in a cool place.

Stance
Stand ten to fifteen yards from the target and gradually move further away as skill develops. Straddle the shooting line with the left side facing the target. Weight is distributed equally on both feet, which are approximately shoulder width apart. Lines drawn horizontally through both heels and the shoulders should converge at the center of the target. Point the toes straight ahead, then turn the head toward the target. The archer should *stand tall* and not lean forward, backward, right, or left.

Holding the Bow
With the bow in a vertical position, arrow rest up, give a left handshake to the handle. (See Figure 1-19) The hand and top of the handle should be even. The index finger wraps around the bow with the thumb resting on the finger. The other fingers are in a relaxed position. The wrist is behind the bow, and the left arm is slightly bent to rotate the elbow down and out, thereby preventing the string from slapping the arm. The correct arm position and an extra long arm guard, that comes above the elbow, will minimize string slap.

Nocking the Arrow

Hold the bow horizontally in the left hand with the string facing you and arrow rest to the thumb side of the hand. With the right hand, hold the arrow at the nock between the thumb and forefinger. Place the arrow on top of the bow and slide into the string at right angles with the cock or odd-colored feather up. Use the index finger of the other hand to steady the arrow until drawing begins. Do not forget to replace the index finger around the handle before shooting. Use a nocking point on the string to insure nocking the arrow at the same place every time. (See Figure 1-20)

Figure 1-19. Holding the Bow.   Figure 1-20. Nocking the Arrow.

Drawing the Bow

The string is drawn by the first three fingers with the arrow between the first and second. The string rests in the first joint of all three fingers. Do not squeeze the nock, as this will cause difficulty in keeping the arrow pile against the bow. (See Figure 1-21)

Rotate the bow leftward from a horizontal to a vertical position and stop with the left arm parallel to the ground. Push the bow away and simultaneously draw the string toward you. The upper arm, shoulder, and upper back muscles are used in a good draw. The archer should feel as though he is drawing his shoulder blades together. Take a deep breath during the draw and hold until after the arrow is released.

Anchoring

The *anchor point* is the spot on the archer's face where the hand is placed at full draw. Target archers generally anchor low or under the chin, while field archers and hunters anchor high on the cheek bone. The low anchor lowers the point of aim in distant shooting while the high anchor brings the arrow point nearer the target.

In the low anchor the forefinger centers under the chin and the string is drawn to the middle of the nose and chin. (See Figure 1-22) The draw arm should be in alignment with the drawn arrow. Avoid tilting the head when anchoring and always be consistent in the anchor point. In the high anchor, the back corner of the mouth serves as the anchor point with the index finger resting just under the cheekbone.

Figure 1-21. Placement of Shooting Fingers On String.

Figure 1-22. Full Draw with Low Anchor Point.

Aiming and Holding

There are three methods of aiming: *point of aim, bow sight,* and *instinctive.* The beginner should use the point of aim method to avoid overdrawing the arrow. After acquiring basic shooting techniques, archers may progress to sight shooting, which is the most accurate shooting method. The most difficult aiming technique is instinctive, or bare bow shooting, in which the archer uses only his experienced judgment in aiming.

Point of Aim. With any given bow and arrow, there is just one distance where a person can aim at the center of the target and hit it. This distance is called *point blank range.* If the archer stands further from the target than this distance and aims at the center, his arrows will fall short. In order to hit the target, the archer must aim above it. If the archer moves closer to the target and aims at the center his arrows will fly over it. He must aim at some object on the ground in front of the target. This object is called the *point of aim.* The point of aim *(P.O.A.)* technique involves sighting the tip of the arrow onto an object on the ground or elsewhere and releasing without looking directly at the target. Remember to aim in front of the target when close, at the target when approximately twenty yards away, and above the target as distance increases. (See Figure 1-23)

To locate the point of aim from the shooting line vertically hold the bow at arm's length with the string passing through the center of the gold. (See Figure 1-24) The point of aim will be along the line of the string. To find the exact point along the string, place a small block of wood on the ground one-third of the distance from the target. Aim at the bottom of the block and shoot several arrows. If they fall low, move the aiming point toward the target. High groupings indicate the need to move the P.O.A. closer to the archer. Keep shooting until several consecutive arrows hit the target. You then know the P.O.A. for that distance. Repeat the procedure for different distances.

To permanently record your P.O.A., use a *range finder*, which may be a tongue depressor with a square corner. (See Figure 1-25) Mark a red dot in the top square corner. Straddle the shooting line, then raise the wooden stick until the red dot in the top corner is lined up with the center of the gold. Look down at your point of aim and mark that spot and distance on the stick. Repeat and record all distances needed.

To use the range finder, stand where you will be shooting and hold the stick at arms length toward the target. Line up the red dot and center of the gold on the target. Look past the range mark on

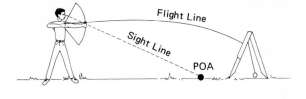

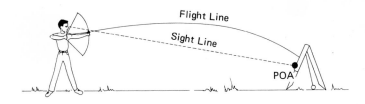

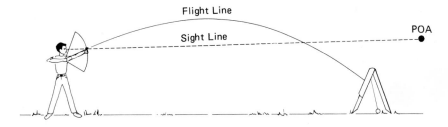

Figure 1-23. P.O.A. Principle for Close Range, Point Blank, and Long Range.

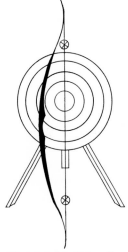

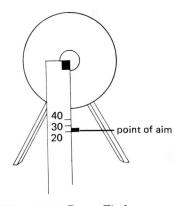

Figure 1-25. Range Finder.

Figure 1-24. Using the
Bowstring to Align
P.O.A. with Gold.

your finder, and the spot where your line of sight hits the ground
will be your P.O.A. (See Figure 1-26)

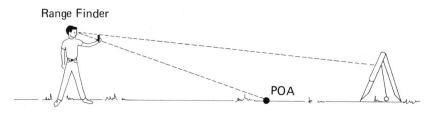

Figure 1-26. Using A Range Finder.

Right-handed shooters aim with the right eye and close the left.
To sight with the right eye, look to the right of the string, left of the
bow, to the tip of the arrow, to the base of the P.O.A. Both eyes
may be opened when shooting if your right eye is dominant. If your
left eye is dominant, you must shoot left-handed or close the left
eye. To increase accuracy when practicing, work toward seeing the
string lined up as close to the left of the bow as possible.

Sight Shooting. Sight shooting involves the use of a mechanical
device which is adjustable vertically and horizontally. (See Figure
1-9) To improve a *sight,* place an eight-inch strip of adhesive and a
small black-headed straight pin on the back of the bow just above the
handle. When aiming place the head of the pin on the gold and shoot
several arrows. Proper placement of the pinhead is found by trial and
error. If arrows are grouped anywhere other than at the center, move
the sight in the direction of the error for correction. If the group is
low and left, move the pin down and to the left.

Instinctive Shooting. An aiming device is not used with instinctive shooting. Keep both eyes open, to develop depth perception,
and focus on the exact center of the gold. Release several arrows and
make bow adjustments up, down, and/or to either side according to
where the arrows fall. Through practice, kinesthetic awareness, visual
awareness, and archery skills must be developed.

No matter what aiming method is selected, all require a holding
position. After the full draw is assumed, it is necessary to concentrate and hold for two or three seconds. Use your back and shoulder
muscles to avoid creeping, permitting the string to move forward
before releasing the arrow.

The Loose or Release

Without moving any other part of your body, relax fingers of the draw hand, allowing the string to slip off the fingers. Attempt to keep the bow at draw level, but permit it to move in its natural position. The release should be smooth, not jerky. The right hand and elbow move straight back past the neck into the follow-through position.

Follow-Through
or After-Hold

Hold the release position until after the arrow lands. Keep looking at the P.O.A., not the flight of the arrow. Analyze each shot by studying the position of the bow hand, elbow, and shoulder and the string hand and elbow. The after-hold position will tell you much about how you shot the arrow. (See Figure 1-27)

Figure 1-27. Release and Follow-Through.

Retrieving Arrows

Place your left hand, palm facing you, on the target face, with the arrow between your index and middle fingers. While pushing against the target with your left hand, grasp the arrow close to the target face with your right hand. Gently twist and pull it straight out. (See Figure 1-28) No one should stand behind the person pulling arrows from the target. Place the drawn arrow in the hand against the target, between the thumb and forefinger, with the crest hanging down. Carry arrows fanned out to prevent feathers from touching. (See Figure 1-29)

To retrieve arrows from the ground, stoop, grasp the arrow as close to the ground as possible and pull straight back. If the feathers are buried in the grass, locate the tip and pull the arrow forward until it is free.

To prevent stepping on arrows on the way to the target, retrieve all you see and place those not belonging to you under the tripod.

Figure 1-28. Retrieving Arrows from the Target.

Figure 1-29. Carrying Arrows.

Never shoot at a target with a *hanging* arrow. Archers stop shooting to permit the person who shot it to walk forward to straighten it.

Common Beginning Errors

To become proficient, the archer must analyze each shot. Determine the placement of each arrow by naming the color and number by thinking of the target as the face of a clock. Work toward grouping the arrows in one location. Be consistent in everything you do and always shoot with the same bow. Some common causes of arrows going high, low, right, or left are diagramed in Figure 1-30.

RULES

Competition In Target Archery

1. Straddle the shooting line.
2. Shoot only on the signal given by the presiding tournament officials; Field Captain for men and Lady Paramount for ladies.
3. Six arrows constitute an *end*. When shooting an end, only six arrows should be shot. If more than six arrows are shot, score the lowest six.

HIGH
1. Lifting bow arm at release.
2. Extension of bow arm on release.
3. "Jerking"—Backward movement of hand before release.
4. Increasing pull of string hand just before releasing arrow.
5. "Peeking"—Looking up when releasing and following flight.
6. P.O.A. too high, close to target, or sight too low.
7. Forefinger of bow hand up so arrow rides high.
8. Anchoring low or with mouth opened.
9. Dropping elbow of string hand.
10. Leaning away from target.
11. Arrow nocked low.
12. Heeling the bow.

LEFT   13. Overdrawing.   RIGHT

1. Hunching left shoulder.
2. Weight on or toward heels.
3. Tilting top of bow to left.
4. Anchoring out from side of face.
5. Bow arm thrown to left at release.
6. Straightening bow arm on release.
7. Failure to align P.O.A. with center of target: too far to left.
8. Head dropped backward rather than rotated to left.
9. Aiming to the left of the bow string.
10. Sighting with wrong (left) eye.

1. Throwing bow arm to right.
2. Plucking string to right.
3. Tilting top of bow to right.
4. Failure to align P.O.A. with center of target: too far to right.
5. Weight on or toward toes.
6. Holding string in too far on string finger.
7. Jerky release.
8. Letting fingers come forward causing the string to roll out around fingers.
9. Left-handed archer sighting with right (wrong) eye.

LOW
1. Holding too long.
2. Right elbow dropping.
3. Leaning toward the target.
4. P.O.A. too low, far from target, or sight too high.
5. "Creeping"—Letting the drawing arm come forward or letting the bow arm bend before releasing.
6. Not bringing arrow to full draw before release.
7. Reaching forward with chin to string.
7. Dropping bow arm at release.
9. Too high an anchor.
10. Arrow nocked high.

Figure 1-30. Causes of Arrows Going Right, Left, High, and Low.

4. Step back three paces after shooting an end.
5. A *round* consists of a number of ends shot at several (usually three) different distances.
6. The longest distance in a round is shot first, progressing to the shortest.
7. Practice is not permitted between rounds.
8. Groups of four people shoot at each target.
   A. Target Captain calls the value of each arrow as he pulls it from the target.
   B. Two scorers score independently and check results after each end and round to avoid errors.
   C. Assistant Captain assists the Captain.

9. Scores are recorded from the highest to the lowest. (See Figure 1-31)
10. The number of hits are recorded.
11. All archers retrieve arrows together and only on command.
12. Arrows must bear a clear and different crest for recognition.

Scoring In Target Archery

1. Values of rings in five-ring scoring are gold, 9; red, 7; blue, 5; black, 3; white; 1. Values in ten-ring scoring are: gold 10,9; red 8,7; blue 6,5; black 4,3; white 2,1.
2. If the arrow bisects two colors, it scores the higher of the two values. An arrow on the line between the red and gold would score 9 points.
3. An arrow in the petticoat, the black line around the white ring and area outside this ring has no scoring value and is not considered a hit.
4. An arrow hitting a target other than the one at which you are shooting does not score.
5. An arrow which rebounds from the scoring face, if witnessed, is seven points if shot from 60 yards or less and five points if shot from more than 60 yards. In either case draw a circle around the score on the score card.
6. An arrow that passes through the target, if witnessed, shall score the same as a rebound. Draw a circle around this score on the score card.
7. An arrow that falls from the bow that can be reached with the bow, is not considered shot and may be shot again. Otherwise it counts zero.
8. An arrow is considered shot if the tackle breaks during shooting.
9. An arrow must be left in the target until scored.
10. In case of a tie, the highest score at the longest distance is the winner.

Commonly Used Rounds

American Round. For men and women fifteen years and up.
　　　5 ends at 60 yards
　　　5 ends at 50 yards
　　　5 ends at 40 yards

Name	Miki Waldman		Joan Leary		Diane Duffy		Vonnie Brown	
Round	Jr. Amer. Round		Jr. Amer. Round		Jr. Amer. Round		Jr. Amer. Round	
Date	June 3, 1971		June 3, 1971		June 3, 1971		June 3, 1971	
	Hits	Score	Hits	Score	Hits	Score	Hits	Score
At 50 yds.	5	31	4	24	6	24	5	35
	6	40	5	33	5	31	5	31
	5	29	6	28	4	14	6	38
	6	36	6	42	6	28	4	22
	6	42	5	29	6	38	6	20
	28	178	26	156	27	135	26	146
At 40 yds.	6	26	5	25	6	42	5	21
	4	10	4	22	6	50	6	34
	3	15	6	30	6	44	6	38
	5	23	5	21	6	36	6	38
	6	40	4	12	6	52	4	20
	24	114	24	116	30	224	27	151
At 30 yds.	6	46	6	46	6	38	6	44
	6	44	6	42	6	52	6	42
	6	54	6	36	6	48	6	38
	6	46	6	30	6	48	6	36
	6	44	5	31	6	42	6	46
	30	234	29	185	30	228	30	206
Total Score	82	526	79	457	87	587	83	503

Team Score 331 - 2073

Figure 1-31. Sample Scoresheet for Five-Ring Scoring.

Junior American Round. For men and women twelve years and up.

> 5 ends at 50 yards
> 5 ends at 40 yards
> 5 ends at 30 yards

Columbia Round. For women twelve years and up.

> 4 ends at 50 yards
> 4 ends at 40 yards
> 4 ends at 30 yards

York Round. For men eighteen years and up.

> 12 ends at 100 yards
> 8 ends at 80 yards
> 4 ends at 60 yards

Team Round For Men. Four archers combined score.

> 16 ends at 60 yards

Team Round For Women. Four archers combined score.

> 16 ends at 50 yards

F.I.T.A. International competition for men.

> 6 ends at 90 meters
> 6 ends at 70 meters
> 6 ends at 50 meters
> 6 ends at 30 meters

F.I.T.A. International competition for women.

> 6 ends at 70 meters
> 6 ends at 60 meters
> 6 ends at 50 meters
> 6 ends at 30 meters

Safety Practices

1. Check all tackle (equipment) before use.
2. Avoid wearing bulky clothing or clothing with pins, buttons, pockets, or ruffles on the left to interfere with the bowstring release.
3. Wear protective equipment.
4. Always treat archery tackle as lethal weapons.
5. When shooting in a group, shoot and recover arrows at one time.
6. Place ground quivers behind the shooting line.
7. In target archery, straddle the shooting line and in field archery, stand at the appropriate stake.

Bow

1. Brace and unbrace the bow correctly.
2. Measure the fistmele; if it is less than 6 inches, string slap may occur.
3. Never release the string of an empty bow at full draw. The bow is more apt to break, since the missing arrow cannot absorb the bow pressure. Slowly permit the string to return to its normal position.
4. Don't overdraw the bow.
5. Always unbrace the bow after shooting.

Arrows

1. Use the correct size and weight.
2. Never point the bow with a nocked arrow anywhere, but at the target.
3. Never show your skill by using a human target or permitting someone to hold a target.

Shooting

1. Check your target for stability before shooting.
,2. Be sure the range is clear before shooting.
3. In target archery, wait for the command to shoot, and in field archery call *timber* prior to shooting.
4. Don't shoot straight up in the air.
5. When you finish shooting, stand in back of the shooting line.
6. One member of your group should stand in front of the target while others are looking for arrows. If alone, leave your bow against the target face.

TERMINOLOGY

Anchor Point—A definite point on the shooter's face where the index finger of the string hand comes to on the draw to give consistency to shooting.

Arm Guard—A device used to protect the bow arm from string abrasions.

Arrow Plate—A substance inlaid on the side of the bow where the arrow crosses to protect the bow from excessive wear.

Arrow Rest—A horizontal shelf on the top of the bow handle on which the arrow rests.

Back—Side of the bow away from the archer when shooting.

Belly—Inside of the bow facing the archer when shooting.

Bow Hand—The hand which holds the bow while shooting.

Bowyer—A bow maker.

Brace—To string the bow.

Broadhead—A large flat hunting head with razor-sharp blades.

Cast—The speed or distance with which the bow shoots an arrow.

Cock Feather—The different colored feather which is set at right angles to the nock.

Composite Bow—A bow made of layers of more than one kind of material.

Creeping—Allowing the string hand to edge forward before or during a release.

Crest—Colored marks near the feathers on an arrow for identification.

Draw—To pull the bowstring back into the shooting position.

End—Six arrows in succession or in two groups of three; in field archery, four arrows.

Fast—An expression used to warn people of arrows being shot.

Field Captain—Man in charge of a tournament.

Fistmele—Distance between the bow handle and string measured from the base of a fist to the tip of the extended thumb, approximately six to seven inches.

F.I.T.A.—Federation Internationale de Tir a l' Arc; this is the international governing body of archery.

Fletcher—A person who makes arrows.

Fletching—The feathers on an arrow.

Free Style—Shooting with the aid of a bow sight.

Group—A cluster of arrows that are in approximately the same place on the target.

Hanging Arrow—An arrow which does not penetrate the face of the target sufficiently to hold it in and hangs from the target face.

Hen Feathers—The two feathers that are not at right angles to the arrow nock.

Hit—An arrow that lands within the scoring area on the target.

Holding—Holding the arrow at full draw before releasing.

Instinctive Shooting—Aiming and shooting without bow sight or point-of-aim method. Often called *bare bow* method.

Lady Paramount—Lady in charge of a tournament.

Loose—To release the bowstring following the draw.

N.A.A.—National Archery Association; this is the official governing body of amateur archery in the United States.

Nock—The deep groove in the end of an arrow; the grooves at either end of the bow which holds the bowstring in place; to place the arrow on the string.

Nocking Point—The marked place on the bow string where the arrow is placed before drawing and releasing.

Overdraw—Unsafe act of drawing the arrow back too far so that the tip passes the handle of the bow.

Petticoat—That part of the target face beyond the white ring; counts as a miss.

Pile—The head, tip, or point of an arrow.

Point-Blank Range—Distance at which the point-of-aim is the center of the gold.

Point-Of-Aim—The point at which one should aim to hit the target. When sighting, the tip of the arrow is at the base of the P.O.A. This allows for trajectory of the arrow.

Quiver—A receptacle for carrying or holding arrows.

Range—Distance to be shot; the shooting area, indoors or out.

Range Finder—A device for determining varying points of aim.

Rebound—An arrow that bounces off the scoring area of the target.

Round—A prescribed number of ends shot at specified distances.

Roving—Shooting at random targets such as stumps, trees, and bushes with unknown and varying distances. Good practice for hunting.

Self—Bow or arrow made of one piece of material.

Serving—The thread wrapped around the bowstring at the nocking point.

Shaft—The main body of an arrow.

Shaftment—The part of the arrow from the nock through the crest.

Sight—A device on the bow enabling the archer to aim directly at the gold.

Spine—Stiffness-flexibility combination of an arrow.

Stabilizer—A weight extending out from the midsection of the bow that helps stabilize the bow.

Tab—A flat piece of leather worn on the shooting hand to protect the fingers from the string.

Tackle—Archery equipment.

Tassel—Cloth used to wipe soiled or wet arrows.

Timber—A warning to others in field archery.

Toxophilite—An ardent student and practitioner of archery.

Trajectory—The path of an arrow in flight.

Weight—The number of pounds required to draw the bowstring the length of its arrow.

BIBLIOGRAPHY

Books

American Association for Health, Physical Education, and Recreation. *Group Archery Instruction For Beginners.* Washington, D.C., 1967.

Athletic Institute. *How To Improve Your Archery.* Chicago, Illinois: The Athletic Institute, 1962.

Barrett, Jean A. *Archery.* Pacific Palisades, California: Goodyear Publishing Company, 1969.

Burke, Edmund. *Archery.* New York: ARC Books, Inc., 1965.

D.G.W.S. Archery-Riding Guide. 1970-72. Washington, D.C.: American Association for Health, Physical Education, and Recreation.

Gillelan, G. Howard. *The Young Sportsman's Guide To Archery.* New York: Thomas Nelson & Sons, 1962.

Keasey, Gilman and Natalie Reichart. *Archery.* (3rd ed.), New York: The Ronald Press Company, 1961.

McCue, Betty F. (Editor) *Physical Education Activities For Women.* "Archery," Toronto, Canada: The Macmillan Company, 1969.

McKinney, Wayne C. *Archery: Physical Education Activities Series.* Dubuque, Iowa: William C. Brown Company Publishers, 1966.

National Archery Association. *The Archer's Handbook.* (2nd ed.), Ronks, Pennsylvania: The National Archery Association Inc. of the United States, 1968.

Niemeyer, Roy K. *Beginning Archery: Wadsworth Sports Skill Series.* Belmont, California: Wadsworth Publishing Company, Inc., 1962.

Vannier, Maryhelen and Hally Beth Poindexter. *Individual and Team Sports for Girls and Women.* (2nd ed.), Philadelphia: W.B. Saunders Co., 1969.

Periodicals

Archery World. Official publication of the National Archery Association of the United States. Boyertown, Pennsylvania: Archer's Magazine Company, 19512.

Bow and Arrow. Gallant Publishing Company, 116 E. Badillo, Covina, California 91722.

Pamphlets

Miller, Myrtle K. *Practical Aids For Archery Instructors In Colleges. . . .* Used for Instructors' Course at Teela-Wooket Archery Camp, Roxbury, Vermont.

Shakespeare Company. *Shakespeare ABC's Of Archery.* Kalamazoo, Michigan.

BADMINTON

BEHAVIORAL OBJECTIVES

1. Under simulated game conditions, given a badminton racket and shuttlecock, the college student will be able to successfully demonstrate (meet all of the essential criteria as specified in the chapter) the following skills:
   a. Forehand grip.
   b. Backhand grip.
   c. High-deep serve.
   d. Short-low serve.
   e. Drive serve.
   f. Underhand clear shot.
   g. Overhead clear shot.
   h. Drive shot.
   i. Smash shot.
   j. Drop shot.
   k. Hairpin shot.
2. The college student will be able to achieve a score of at least 75 per cent on a written examination concerned with the history, terminology, strategy, rules and analysis of badminton fundamentals.

HISTORY OF BADMINTON

Badminton appears to be a descendant of both the ancient Chinese noncompetitive game of *battledore* (as evidenced by pottery relics and drawings), and a game called *Poona* that developed in India during the middle of the nineteenth century. British army officers, returning from India, introduced Poona to England. Badminton derives its name from the famous estate in Gloucestershire, England, where it developed as an outgrowth of both battledore and Poona during the early 1870's.

Consistent with the development of many games and sports, a need arose to establish a standardized set of playing rules, and to foster the game in other countries. Consequently, during the 1890's, organizations such as the Badminton Association of England and the National Badminton Association of America (now called the American Badminton Association) were formed. As interest and proficiency in badminton increased, a need also arose for both national and international tournament play. The Thomas Cup (men) and the Uber Cup (women) represent forms of international competition that invoke pride both in the individual player and the country represented.

NATURE OF BADMINTON

Badminton is a relatively easy game to learn, and can be played by men and women of all ages. It is played with rackets and a shuttlecock (bird or shuttle) on a court divided by a net, by either two (singles) or four people (doubles), and can be played both indoors and outdoors. The shuttle is hit over the net, and all returns must be made before the shuttle lands in the designated court area. (See Figure 2-1) Since the shuttle is hit on a fly, badminton is an extremely fast court game, requiring of the advanced player enormous concentration, quick reflexes, and superb conditioning.

The basic objective of a particular play or rally is to win the point. This is accomplished by deceptively employing a wide variety of well-executed strokes that allow you to hit and place the shuttle so well, that the opponent is forced into error. However, points can only be scored by the serving side; if the receiving side wins the rally, they then receive the service. A game consists of a minimum of 15 points, except ladies' singles which consists of 11 points. If a game becomes tied at 13-all or 14-all (9-all or 10-all in ladies' singles), the player or team reaching either of these points first has the option of *setting* the score; play then continues until a player or team wins the number of points set. The best of three games constitutes a match. The initial choice before the first game of a particular side, or the right to serve, or to receive, is decided by tossing. Players switch sides of the court after each game; if there is a third game, players switch sides again after 8 points (15 point game), or 6 points (11 point game). The winning player or team serves first the next game.

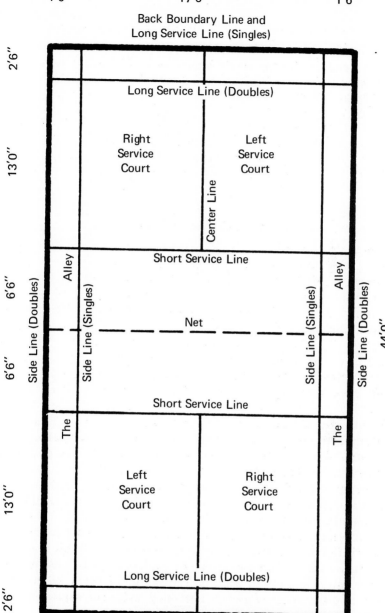

Figure 2-1. Badminton Court.

EQUIPMENT

The equipment needed to play badminton is relatively inexpensive. The easy handling of the light-weight racket, as well as the unique structure of the shuttle, make badminton an interesting and enjoyable game to play. (Figure 2-2)

Figure 2-2. Racket and Shuttlecock.

Racket

The badminton racket is light (5-5 1/2 oz) and easy to maneuver. The frame is usually made of wood, with a steel or fiberglass shaft. The handle usually contains a leather or rubber grip; grip circumference sizes vary from 3 inches (small) to 4 inches (large), with the smaller grip size usually corresponding to a lighter weight racket. Choice of grip size, racket weight, and racket balance, is often an individual preference that comes from playing experience. The racket head can be strung with nylon or gut, and at various tensions. There are also different qualities of both nylon and gut. Nylon is less expensive than gut, is more resistant to moisture, and consequently, probably more feasible in a school setting. However, it is generally believed that gut provides greater resiliency and is consequently more desirable for tournament play. In choosing a racket, primary consideration should first be given toward the frame, i.e., the strings can always be replaced. As a general rule, the more laminations (ply) a racket head has and the thinner they are, the better is the quality of the racket. A racket should also be kept in a press to prevent moisture from causing the racket head to warp.

Shuttlecock

The introduction of plastic and nylon shuttles has helped eliminate some of the wear-and-tear problems of feathered *shuttles*, especially in school and club settings. Nevertheless, the feathered type of shuttle is used for regular tournament play, even though it is the most expensive and requires the most care. Shuttles vary in their speed—slow, medium, and fast; the heavier the shuttle, the faster it travels. A shuttle weighs from 73 to 85 grains and has 14-16 feathers attached to a cork base. It is obvious then that differences in shuttle weight can affect the nature of the game played. Shuttle speed will also vary according to court temperature, humidity, and altitude. Therefore, preliminary to a tournament contest, the rules provide for a test of the shuttle to determine and standardize shuttle pace. Shuttles should always be properly stored according to specified humidity conditions, and handled with care.

In addition to a racket and shuttlecock, a net and net posts are all that are required to play badminton.

SKILLS* TO BE DEVELOPED

The Grip

Gripping the racket properly helps to ensure a more effective badminton stroke. The grip should be relatively firm for power strokes, and more relaxed for delicate touch shots. The racket should be held so that the heel of the hand extends down to the butt of the handle. The grip should feel comfortable, and it may be helpful to adjust the amount of finger spread on the handle. Also, a comfortable racket handle size is an important feature to consider when buying a badminton racket. When a shuttle is stroked from the right side of the body (forehand side), and for most overhead strokes, the forehand grip is used. When the shuttle is stroked from the left side of the body (backhand side), the backhand grip is used (except for the advanced round-the-head stroke), and the shuttle is contacted on the opposite face of the racket as that of the forehand stroke.

Forehand Grip. (See Figure 2-3) Grip the racket so that the racket head is perpendicular to the floor, i.e., "shake hands" with the racket handle. When the racket is held in this perpendicular position, the point of the "V" formed by the thumb and forefinger of your right hand should appear on the top plane of the eight-sided racket handle. The handle lies diagonally across the fingers and palm. The

---

*All instructions are geared to the right-handed player; left-handed players should reverse the directions.

fingers are very slightly spread (the forefinger and third finger may be somewhat more apart), the thumb is wrapped around the handle, and the little finger is anchored against the butt of the handle. The beginner should avoid the *Western grip* (gripping the racket so that the racket head is parallel rather than perpendicular to the floor), as this is a less efficient forehand grip, and it is also more difficult to switch to the backhand grip.

Backhand Grip. (See Figure 2-4) If the above forehand grip is used to hit a backhand stroke, the shuttle will most likely tend to fly

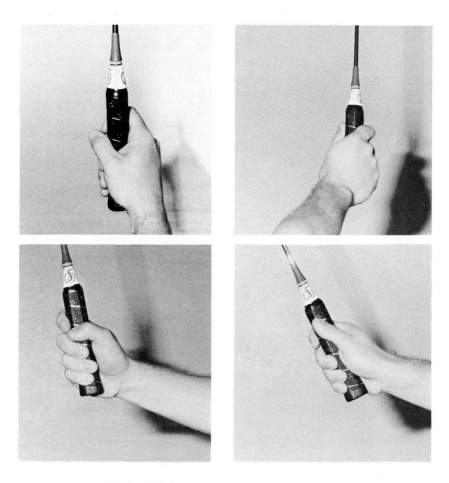

Figure 2-3. Forehand Grip.   Figure. 2-4. Backhand Grip.

upwards, *setting up* your opponent. Consequently, when hitting a backhand stroke it is desirable to slightly close the racket face to the point of contact of the shuttle. This can be accomplished by turning your right hand to the left or counterclockwise about one-eighth of the circumference of the racket handle. The "V" now appears on the top left plane of the handle, and for power strokes, your thumb can be placed against the back plane.

Many advanced players prefer to use one grip for both forehand and backhand strokes, since they cannot afford the time to switch grips. Consequently, they employ a compromise grip, midway between the backhand and forehand grips. This grip also allows you to contact the shuttle in the overhead position with a more open face, thereby deceptively slowing down the speed of the shuttle.

A related feature of the grip is the important concept of "wrist action." The racket is cocked back (hyperextended) at the end of the backswing of a stroke, and then the wrist is snapped (flexed) into the shuttle at the contact point of the forward swing. This is especially important for deception and where power is desired. To achieve this wrist action, both the correct grip and a flexible wrist are essential.

The Serve

The initial stroke of each point in a game is the serve. The badminton serve can be considered a defensive stroke in that the rules require you to serve underhand. In addition, only one serve is permitted per point. However, the serve can be made a potent offensive weapon by skillfully employing control, deception, and a variety of serving strategies. To achieve this end, your objective when serving should be to prevent the receiver from making an offensive return by forcing him off balance. This goal is a realistic one, for you have more time than any other stroke to hit the shuttle. It is vital that this goal be achieved, for it is only when serving that you can score points.

The position you take on the court to serve may vary, depending on whether you are playing singles or doubles. The forehand grip is most often used, although it is permissible to serve underhand backhand (but rarely used). The serving stance is approximately shoulder width apart, knees are slightly flexed, and left foot in front of right. When serving to the right service court your stance is slightly open to the net, whereas when serving to the left service court your stance is slightly closed to the net. The racket is held behind your body with the handle at about waist height, and the racket head higher. The wrist is cocked and ready for action, and the elbow is slightly bent. This is the starting position. (See Figure 2-5a)

Dropping the shuttle correctly is an important facet of serving. The cork end of the shuttle should be held loosely between the thumb and forefinger of the left hand. Avoid holding the shuttle by the feathers, as this may prevent it from falling straight down. The left arm should be slightly flexed at the elbow, away from the body, and at about shoulder height. The shuttle should be dropped well out in front of, and slightly to the right of, your body. Beginners should not attempt to toss the shuttle on the release, as this will cause some loss of control and consistency.

The shuttle is released and this simultaneously initiates the forward swing. The racket is brought forward in an underhand motion. Power is obtained by shifting your body weight forward, rotating your body inward, and applying wrist action in conjunction with forward arm motion. Contact is made diagonally in front of your left foot and slightly above knee level. (See Figure 2-5b) The follow-through represents a natural continuation of the forward swing (See figure 2-5c), and will vary according to the type of serve employed.

There are three basic variations of the serve—*The short-low, high-deep,* and *drive serves.* While each serve differs in speed, trajectory, and court placement, it is crucial that they appear indistinguishable in form until contact is almost made. The server can then effectively employ deception.

a. starting position   b. contact point   c. follow-through

Figure 2-5. The Serve.

The High-Deep Serve. The high-deep serve is used most often in singles, as the long service line for singles is the back boundary line. The shuttle should reach an apex of about twenty feet or higher, and fall perpendicular and as close to the back boundary line as possible. In doubles, a lower and shorter variation of this serve is sometimes used against a receiver who plays too close to the short service line. However, the high-deep serve is most effective in singles, since it may nullify even a smash, by forcing the receiver to hit from the back boundary line. The shuttle should preferably be placed to the receiver's backhand side, although it may also sometimes be placed to the forehand side, as a change of pace. (See Figure 2-6) The follow-through of the high-deep serve finishes high above the left (opposite) shoulder.

The Short-Low Serve. This serve is used more often in doubles than the higher serve, since the service court is wider but shorter. The shuttle should just barely clear the net and land in the receiver's short backhand service court corner; for a change of pace the serve may also travel to the receiver's forehand side. (See Figure 2-6) The emphasis here is on delicate control, rather than on power. The follow-through of the short-low serve is slower and more toward the

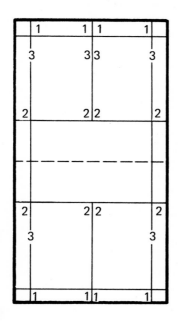

1. High—Deep
2. Short—Low
3. Drive

Figure 2-6. Serve Placements.

net than the high-deep serve, because of reduced elevation and momentum at contact.

The Drive Serve. The drive serve, though slightly more difficult to execute, is extremely effective as a surprise serve. The shuttle speed is rapid, the trajectory is horizontal to the floor, and the shuttle should pass low over the net. Emphasis here is on placement, and the shuttle can be directed to an unguarded area of the receiver's service court, or directly at his body. (See Figure 2-6) The danger of this serve is that it could be very rapidly returned by the receiver if it is not properly placed. The follow-through of the drive serve is also toward the net, but is more rapid than the short serve.

In all three variations of the serve, deception and power are basically differentiated by the amount of sudden wrist action at the contact point. Shuttle trajectory is governed by the angle of the racket face at contact. Shuttle placement is influenced by such factors as the angle position of the racket face at contact, forward racket momentum, and the direction of the follow-through.

The Clear Shot

The clear is an important defensive stroke in badminton, and is sometimes even effective as an offensive stroke. The clear can be hit from either underhand or overhead positions (more advanced players also employ a round-the-head clear), and from forehand or backhand sides. Consequently, either forehand or backhand grips may be appropriate. As a defensive stroke, the purpose of the clear is to hit the shuttle high enough, and far enough, so that you have enough time to regain court position. Ideally the shuttle should fall perpendicular to the back boundary line.

Hitting a clear from the overhead position is more desirable than from the underhand position in that you can apply more power to the stroke, and therefore keep the shuttle deep. In addition, hitting from the overhead position forces you to swing sooner, giving your opponent less time to set up. The forehand overhead clear is more frequently used than the backhand overhead clear since the former is a more powerful stroke, especially from the backcourt.

In hitting any overhead stroke (once you have moved into position), your body should be sideways to the net, with your left foot ahead of your right. Your weight is evenly distributed on both feet. As the shuttle approaches, your weight shifts back to your right foot, while your racket is brought back parallel to the floor past your right ear. At the completion of this backswing, your weight is on your right foot, your back slightly arched, your racket cocked behind your back with right arm bent, and your left arm fully extended in the direction of the shuttle to help ensure perfect timing and positioning. (See Figure 2-7a)

The strategy of the forward swing of the overhead stroke is analogous to that of the serve. In both cases deception is extremely important. However, in the forehand overhead clear, this may not strictly apply when used as a defensive stroke. There will be somewhat more knee flexion, as an attempt is made to swing forward and upward to hit the falling shuttle, while the weight is shifted forward. The shuttle is contacted in front of the body with the arm fully extended. (See Figure 2-7b) Wrist action is imparted for additional power. There is very little follow-through since the swing was forward and upward. (See Figure 2-7c)

a. backswing   b. contact point   c. follow through

Figure 2-7. Overhead Clear Shot.

The overhead clear can be made into a more offensive stroke by reducing the height and controlling the power of the shuttle. The purpose of this stroke is to send the shuttle behind your opponent, and to force him off balance and out of position. Most clears should be aimed to your opponent's backhand side. The underhand clear is quite similar in form to the high-deep serve, with the main exception being that you must first move into position; rather than dropping the shuttle yourself, you must time your swing so as to meet the shuttle diagonally in front of your body.

The Smash Shot

While the clear can be considered a key defensive stroke, the smash is definitely the most potent offensive stroke of the game. Enormous power is generated into the shuttle, and a well-placed smash should be a sure point against any opponent. The most prevalent smash is from the forehand overhead position, although a backhand smash (when near the net), and the advanced round-the-head smash can also be used.

As opposed to the clear, the trajectory of the smash is down. Consequently, the taller player probably has the advantage in terms of being able to hit down with a greater angle. However, fully extending your racket arm at contact (and sometimes even by jumping), allows you to take full advantage of your height. As in the clear, it is important for you to be sideways when smashing, so as to take advantage of body rotation and weight transfer. The grip is firm, and the backswing is similar to the clear. (See Figure 2-7a) During the forward swing, maximal power is obtained by: (1) wrist action, (2) arm swing, (3) inward body rotation, (4) extension of the back which had been arched, and (5) forward weight transfer. Contact is made with the racket arm fully extended and well out in front of your body, and the face of the racket is angled down. (See Figure 2-8a) The follow-through of the smash is downward to the opposite side of your body, and represents a natural continuation of the powerful forward swing. (See Figure 2-8b)

a. contact point   b. follow-through

Figure 2-8. The Smash Shot.

Since more power is generated into the smash than any other stroke, recovery after the follow-through may be momentarily delayed until balance is restored. Therefore, the importance of a well-placed smash is apparent, especially if hitting from the back court. In addition, you can take more chances when smashing in doubles, since your partner may be able to cover for your mistakes. Common mistakes made by the beginner include facing the net when smashing, and inappropriate timing. To achieve maximal power, it is vital that the different components of the forward swing be properly coordinated. In addition, as you get closer to the net, more wrist action is necessary to prevent the shuttle from going beyond the back boundary line.

The Drop Shot

While the clear and smash are basically geared to a back court game, the drop shot enables you to maneuver your opponent in toward the net. The drop shot can be hit from either underhand or overhead positions, and from backhand or forehand sides. The overhead position (especially the forehand side), has the advantage of providing you with the option of either smashing or using the drop shot. The underhand drop shot is used often when returning a smash, but it has the disadvantage of forcing you to hit up on the shuttle. The danger of hitting the drop shot lies in its slow speed. Unless you keep the shuttle extremely low when it passes the net and in the forecourt, your opponent may have time to rush up and smash your drop shot attempt. Therefore, the importance of deception becomes obvious.

The form of the backswing for the overhead drop shot is the same as the smash and the clear. (See Figure 2-7a) The forward swing should also appear the same as the clear and smash. However, momentarily before contacting the shuttle, there should be a sudden slow-down in the arm motion of the swing, thereby imparting less speed to the shuttle. (See Figure 2-9a) Wrist action is important in terms of direction. The follow-through, although to the opposite side of the body, is not as great as the smash because of the reduced momentum of the forward swing. (See Figure 2-9b) The underhand drop shot is similar in form to the low serve, and should therefore be kept as low as possible when passing the net.

The main points to emphasize when practicing the drop shot are control and deception. It is important not to overuse the drop shot, for your opponent will merely become more adept at anticipating your stroke. Beginners should also avoid jabbing or pushing the shut-

a. contact point   b. follow-through

Figure 2-9. The Drop Shot.

tle rather than stroking it, for this reduces its effectiveness as a
surprise stroke, and makes the drop shot less efficient. The drop shot
is not used as often in doubles, especially not against opponents
using an up-and-back strategy system.

When contrasting the offensive overhead clear, smash, and overhead drop shot, it is apparent that to achieve maximum deception,
the form of these strokes should appear almost indistinguishable until contact is made. Differences in shuttle trajectory are caused by
differences in the angle of the face of the racket at the point of
contact. This angle is determined by the trajectory of the forward
swing, the amount of wrist flexion, and the position of the shuttle
relative to the body at the point of contact. Differences in shuttle
speed represent basically, differences in arm momentum and wrist
action, and these differences are sudden so as to create maximum
deception.

The Drive Shot

The drive is a sidearm stroke, hit from either forehand or backhand sides. The purpose of the drive is to draw your opponent out of

position, and to force him to make a defensive return. Sometimes, if enough deception and speed are employed, the drive can win the point. The trajectory of the shuttle is horizontal to the floor, and it should pass low over the net. Contact is made at approximately shoulder level, and well out in front of your body. (See Figure 2-10)

During the backswing of the forehand drive, the racket is rapidly brought back behind your body, with the elbow quite bent and the wrist cocked. The hitting side of the racket face should be open (facing upward) during the backswing, as opposed to the overhead stroke backswing which had a closed racket face during the backswing. Your body is sideways to the net, left foot ahead of right. During the forward swing of the forehand drive (See Figure 2-10a), great power is obtained by the sudden full extension of the racket arm, as well as simultaneous weight shift, body rotation, and wrist action. To hit the shuttle cross-court rather than down the line, more wrist snap as well as greater follow-through are necessary. The crucial point to remember when directing the shuttle is the angle of the face of the racket at the point of contact. Therefore, the cross-court placement is ensured not only by greater wrist flexion, but by contacting the shuttle earlier than the down the line drive.

The backhand drive (See Figure 2-10b) resembles the forehand drive except that there is less body rotation (since your right arm is

a. forehand drive   b. backhand drive

Figure 2-10. The Drive Shot.

now closer to the net than on the forehand drive, and there is no need to turn your body out of the way during the forward swing), less wrist action, and probably more elbow snap. The backhand drive is not as powerful as the forehand drive, and should therefore be avoided when hitting from the back court. The drive is especially effective against an up-and-back doubles team, since quick placements can be made down the alleys. The beginner should avoid over-hitting the drive when near the net.

The Hairpin Shot

The hairpin stroke is an extremely effective net shot that requires great control and touch. Ideally, the shuttle should travel almost straight up, just tip the net, and fall perpendicular on your opponent's side of the court very close to the net. The shuttle can be hit from either the forehand (See Figure 2-11a) or backhand sides. (See Figure 2-11b)

The grip is more relaxed to aid in control and touch. There is relatively little weight shift, body rotation, or arm swing. Most of the power and deception of this stroke is obtained by wrist action. A great deal of practice is necessary to learn how much wrist action to

a. forehand hairpin   b. backhand hairpin

Figure 2-11. The Hairpin Shot.

use for each particular shot. The shuttle should be contacted as near the top of the net as possible, especially since this then gives your opponent little time to return the stroke. If hit successfully, your opponent may be forced to either defensively clear short, hit the net with his racket, or perhaps even miss the shuttle. However, if the hairpin stroke is hit too high and/or without deception, your opponent may be ready to demonstrate his smash to you.

These skills—serve, overhead strokes, drive, and hairpin, are basic to badminton. Once you develop proficiency in these strokes, several more advanced strokes can be added to your repertoire such as round-the-head, angled net shots, hairpin chop, and overhead slice.

Singles Strategy

Complementary to the learning of badminton strokes is the parallel development of an operating plan that forms the basis of what is defined as *strategy*. In playing a dual game such as badminton, where one direct objective is winning, it is essential to have planned moves rather than to stroke and move aimlessly. Yet these planned moves should not be so structured that one cannot adapt to changing patterns of play.

It is important to be in excellent physical condition when playing badminton, for the game requires quick reflexes, sudden stop-and-go movement, and a great deal of running (especially in singles). It is sad to feel that you lost the third game because you were just too tired. Psychologically, fatigue can stifle the drive to win.

Your objective in singles should be to maneuver your opponent in and out, aiming most often to parts of the court not covered. Try to make your opponent's backhand vulnerable to your offensive strokes. The shuttle can be hit cross-court or down the line, short or deep; hitting to mid court is rarely desirable. When warming up with your opponent before a match, try to evaluate his weaknesses. During play, use this knowledge to help win points. Try to anticipate what your opponent is expecting and then give him just the opposite placement. Get into position as quickly as possible so that you can stroke the shuttle with your body well balanced. Hit your high-deep serves near the back boundary line; when your opponent is anticipating this serve, hit either a short-low or drive serve as a change of pace. Always use deception when stroking the shuttle.

Be careful of "letting up" or "choking." Many players when ahead, tend to take it easy or change their strategy. Often, this pattern results in losing points and reinstalling your opponent's confidence. When the game is close, use the strategy that has been most effective in winning points; don't suddenly start practicing new strokes or making wild placements. Use the audience (if there is one) to your advantage, rather than letting them determine the pattern of play. For in singles, you alone are responsible for victory or defeat. In short, a psychologically healthy strategy is of utmost importance to winning play.

Doubles Strategy

In doubles, effective teamwork is the key to winning play. A great deal of practice is needed before each team member knows his responsibility and that of his partner, during each pattern of play. Some of the best singles players in the world, when teamed together, would not necessarily be a top doubles team because of the different strategies doubles entails. In doubles, you have to learn to set up your partner if he is in a better position for the kill, and you have to avoid making your partner vulnerable because of your careless shots. Often, a weakness in a player's game can be offset by effective team positioning. There are probably less clears and more smashes used in doubles, as well as less deception but more hard hitting. A poor smash may not be as risky as in singles, especially if your partner is able to cover for your mistake. There are several strategy systems used in doubles, the most common being the up-and-back, and side-by-side systems.

Up-and-Back System. (See Figure 2-12) This strategy system is an extremely effective offensive pattern. One player (X_1) is positioned in the middle of the fore court, and his partner (X_2) is positioned in

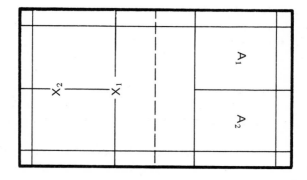

Figure 2-12. Doubles Strategy.

the back court area. The server of the "side-in" team becomes the front man after service. His partner covers the back court. The receiver of the "side-out" team usually comes up after receiving service, while his partner covers the back court; sometimes if the receiver has to move back for a high serve, it may be more advantageous for his partner to then play the front court position. The player up front is responsible for short returns and must cover the entire width of the fore court. His partner is responsible for all shots in the back court and usually takes most mid-court returns. The system is basically an offensive system because the player up front can force the opponents into more rapid play. In addition, this player is in excellent position to hit short, long, and angled kills, as well as skillfully employ the hairpin shot. His partner should try when possible to smash from the back court, so as to force the opponents to hit up and short. The back court man should avoid hitting the clear and drop shot, as this may make his partner vulnerable to the smash. This system is used effectively in mixed doubles, since the women can use touch and control up front.

The weakness of this system lies in its defensive capacity. The man up front is vulnerable to smashes, the alleys are not covered well, and a shuttle placed mid court may cause confusion between the two players. Consequently, when on the defense it is more effective for these players to rotate into a side-by-side system.

Side-by-Side System. (See Figure 2-12) This strategy is an effective defensive system, but lacks strong offensive potential. Both players (A_1, A_2) initially position themselves about mid court, and parallel to each other. Each player is responsible for his length of the court that has been divided by the center line. The alleys are now well covered, and there should not be much confusion when returning a shot that was hit down the middle (the player with the stronger stroke usually makes the return). Players can now also return most smashes if they respond quickly enough.

However, this system lacks offensive potential because the players are too far back to effectively utilize the smash as a kill. They are also vulnerable to drop shots and net shots. These players cannot force their opponents to respond quickly, because their distance from the net has increased, and therefore the shuttle has time to slow down.

The important point to remember is that these systems should be flexible to changing patterns of play. While it is this author's philosophy that offense is the key to winning, the players should nevertheless be ready to drop back into a side-by-side system to better respond defensively.

Serving

Although the serve may be considered a defensive stroke because of its inherent underhand nature, it can be developed into a potent offensive weapon by adherence to the following points:

1. Initial emphasis should be on learning the correct form and placement of the high-deep, short-low, and drive serves.
2. Use of these different serves should vary according to the type of game played (singles or doubles), and the opponent's weaknesses.
3. Deception is a major contributor to an offensive serve. Consequently, the preliminary actions for each of these serves should appear as similar as possible; if this disguise is not maintained, the receiver can anticipate the delivery.
4. The server should be cognizant of the receiver's position and weight distribution. For example, if the receiver has prematurely shifted his weight forward, a high-deep serve may be particularly effective, especially in singles.
5. In singles, the server (X_1, X_2) should position himself to most effectively utilize the high-deep serve, as well as be able to return to the center court position as rapidly as possible after service. Consequently, many servers stand approximately 3-4′ behind the short service line, and close to the center line. (See Figure 2-13a, b)
6. In doubles, the server (X_3) should position himself to most effectively utilize the short-low serve. Consequently, he should stand about 2-3′ behind the short service line and close to the center line, especially when using an up-and-back strategy system. (See Figure 2-13c) In addition, the server's partner (X) can cover for possible deep or wide returns. When utilizing the drive serve in doubles, and when a side-by-side strategy system is employed, it may be helpful to serve from the sideline (X_4), especially when serving from the right service court, since the receiver's backhand is consequently more vulnerable. (See Figure 2-13d)
7. At the completion of the service, the server should be immediately prepared to take the ready position.

Receiving

The basic objective in receiving service is to convert the opponent's serve into an offensive return. The following points may help achieve this objective:

1. The receiver should be cognizant both of his own position within the service court, as well as the position of his opponent.

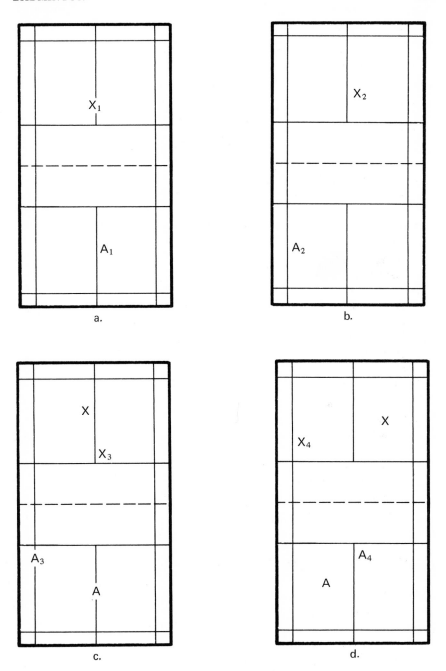

Figure 2-13. Serving and Receiving Positions.

2. The receiving stance should be sideways to the net, rather than facing the net, as this will allow the receiver to most effectively utilize the overhead strokes.

3. In singles, the receiver (A_1, A_2) should be alert to the strong possibility of a high-deep serve, as well as a possible short-low or drive serve. Consequently, the receiver should be about 5' behind the short service line, and when returning from the right service court, as close to the center line as possible. (See Figure 2-13a) When returning from the left service court, the receiver should be close to the singles side line so as to protect his backhand, but should be wary of a possible drive serve down the center line. (See Figure 2-13b)

4. In doubles, the receiver (A_3, A_4) should be as close to the short service line as possible, so as to hit down on any short-low serves. However, he must also be prepared for a possible drive or high score. (See Figure 2-13c, d)

5. After a return is made, the receiver should immediately move to the center position and be prepared for the next possible return.

6. While the receiver should be alert and ready, he should also be poised. He should not be overanxious and charge a serve prematurely, thereby possibly overhitting or hitting the shuttle into the net. In addition, the receiver cannot move until the server has contacted the shuttle during service.

TERMINOLOGY

A.B.A.—American Badminton Association; this is the national governing body of badminton in the United States.

Ace—A point won on which a player completely misses a shuttle in play with his racket.

Alley—A 1 1/2 ft. wide area extending from both singles side lines, that enlarges the court for doubles play.

Back Alley—The area between the long service line (doubles) and the back boundary line.

Back Court—The general area of the court near the back boundary lines.

Back-room—Usually refers to the amount of running space behind the back boundary line.

Balk—Throwing an opponent off balance by using false starts before or during a service attempt.

Band—The canvas tape across the top of the badminton net.

Bird—A shuttlecock.

Block—Placing the racket in front of the shuttle and letting the shuttle rebound into the opponent's court; it is not a stroke.

Carry—An illegal procedure in which the shuttle is momentarily held on the racket during the execution of a stroke.

Center Position—In singles, this position is in the center of the court; in doubles, this position is the center of the court area which the player is covering.

Cross-court—Hitting the shuttle diagonally to the opposite side of the court.

Cross Strings—The horizontal strings of a racket.

Double Hit—An illegal procedure in which the shuttle is hit twice in succession on the same stroke.

Doubles—A game in which there are two people on each side.

End—A side of a badminton court.

Face—The hitting surface of the racket.

Fault—Any violation of the rules, or a playing error.

Flat—The angle of the face of the racket that does not impart spin to the shuttle. Can also refer to the horizontal flight of the shuttle, parallel to the floor.

Flight—The path of the shuttle as it moves through the air.

Fore Court—The general area of the court close to the net.

Frame—The part of the racket which holds the strings.

Game Bird—The game winning point.

Good—A shot which lands within the proper playing area.

Hand-in—Term of service of a player or team.

Hand-out—The loss of service by the serving player or team.

Head—The upper part of the frame, above the throat, which contains the strings.

Head-room—The space above the court which is free from obstructions.

Kill—A smash that an opponent cannot return.

Let—The replaying of a point.

Lob—A clear.

Love—Zero, i.e., zero points for a player or team.

Love-all—No score in the game. It can also indicate the score after a game has been set.

Match—The best two-out-of-three games.

Match Point—The last point needed by the server to win the match.

Mid Court—The general area of the court halfway between the net and either back boundary line.

Net Cord—The upper support of the net. Can also refer to a shot that hits the top of the net and passes into the opponent's court.

No Shot—The term used immediately after hitting an illegal sling, throw, or carry shot.

One Out—Indicates that one member of a doubles team has had his turn at service.

Open Up Court—Leaving an area of the court unprotected.

Overhit—To hit a shuttle with an unnecessarily excessive amount of force, often causing it to travel beyond the back boundary line.

Pass—To hit a shuttle to either side of, and out of reach of, an opponent.

Place—To aim a shot so that it lands in an intended court area.

Point—The unit of scoring in badminton.

Rally—The continuous play during a point.

Ready Position—The initial body position before the beginning of a stroke.

Recover—To make a return of an opponent's well-hit shot.

Retrieve—Same as *Recover.*

Second Service—Same as *One Out.*

Setting—Changing the number of points required to win a game.

Set Up—A poor shot which makes an easy kill for the opponent.

Shaft—The part of the racket between the grip (handle) and the throat.

Short—A shot that fails to reach its mark during play.

Side-in—The side whose turn it is to serve.

Side-out—When the *Side-in* loses serve and becomes the receiving player or team.

Side-room—The space to the side of the court which is free from obstructions.

Stroke—Hitting movement of the racket.

Throat—The part of the racket where the shaft joins the head.

Touching the Net—A fault whereby one touches the net with racket or body.

Wide—A shot that lands out of the court beyond the side boundaries.

Wood Shot—A legal shot (1963) in which the shuttle contacts the frame of the racket, rather than the strings, during the stroke.

RULES

The following is a brief summary of badminton rules or laws. Complete official rules, as well as interpretations and revisions of these rules, can be obtained from either the American Badminton Association or the International Badminton Federation.

Players

1. Either two (singles) or four (doubles) players can participate in a match.

Playing Court (See Figure 2-1)

1. In singles, the proper service court is that area surrounded by the back boundary line, side line (singles), center line, and short service line. Once the serve is in play, the proper court area is encompassed by the back boundary line, side lines (singles), and the net.
2. In doubles, the proper service court is that area surrounded by the long service line (doubles), side line (doubles), center line, and short service line. Once the serve is in play, the proper court area is encompassed by the back boundary line, side lines (doubles), and the net.

Equipment (See Equipment)

Match

1. A match (singles or doubles) consists of the best of three games.
2. A men's singles game consists of a minimum of 15 points, whereas a ladies' singles game consists of a minimum of 11 points. A doubles game consists of a minimum of 15 points.
3. A point can only be scored by the serving side. Play is started by an underhand serve; if the exchange or rally is won by the serving side, a point is recorded. If the receiving side wins this rally, neither side is awarded a point. Instead, the receiving side wins the right to serve and score.

Setting

1. In a 15 point game, if the game becomes tied at 13-all, the side reaching 13 points first has the option of setting that game to 5 points (i.e., the first side to consequently win 5 points would win that game). However, the side may choose not to set the game at 13-all, but rather to play the conventional game of 15 points. If the score then becomes tied at 14-all, the side reaching 14 points first has the option of either setting that game to 3 points, or of merely playing the one additional point required to complete the game.
2. In an 11 point game (ladies' singles), a score tied at 9-all or 10-all can be set to 3 points or 2 points, respectively.

Choice of Serve or Side

1. The winner of the toss (racket or coin) has the choice of either serving, receiving, or defending a particular side.
2. The loser of the toss has the choice of the remaining alternatives.
3. Players change sides of the court at the end of each game. If a third game is necessary, players should again change sides when either player(s) reaches 8 points in a 15 point game, or 6 points in an 11 point game.
4. The winning player or team of the preceding game serves first in the next game. In doubles, either of the two winners may serve first and either of the two losers may receive first, when a new game begins. When the serving side loses an exchange or rally, they become the receiving side. Thereafter, both members of a serving team must be given the right to serve, before the team can become the receiving side.
5. In singles, when the server has an even number of points (e.g., 0, 2, 4, etc.), the serve and receiving of the serve must come from the right service court. If the server has an odd number of points, the serve must be made from the left service court into the diagonally opposite left service court of the receiver.
6. In doubles, when their score is an even number of points, partners should be in the courts (right or left service court) in which they began the game. These court positions are reversed if the team has an odd number of points.

Serving

Violation of any of the following rules by the server constitutes a *fault*, and loss of service.

1. On the serve, the shuttle must be contacted below the server's waist. In addition, the racket head must be below the server's hand holding the racket, when contacting the shuttle.
2. The shuttle must travel over the net and land within the boundaries of the opponent's proper service court. (All lines are good.)
3. If the shuttle hits the top of the net, and lands in the proper service court, it is in play and not a *let.*
4. Preliminary to, or during the service, the server cannot balk.
5. The server cannot step over or touch any boundary line of the service court until after contacting the shuttle during the service.
6. The server must have both feet in contact with the floor until after hitting the shuttle.
7. The server cannot hit the shuttle more than once during the execution of the serve.

8. It is not a fault if the server misses the shuttle completely on the serve.

Receiving

Violations of any of the following rules by the receiver constitutes a *fault*, and loss of the point.

1. The receiver must stand within the proper service court and with both feet in contact with the ground, until the server has contacted the shuttle during service.
2. Preliminary to, or during the service, the receiver cannot balk.
3. Only the intended receiver can return the serve (doubles).
4. The receiver cannot hit the shuttle twice in succession when returning the serve.

Rallying

Violations of any of the following rules by a player during an ensuing rally, is deemed a *fault*.

1. The shuttle must pass over the net and into the proper court area.
2. A shuttle that hits the top of the net and lands in the proper court area is still in play.
3. A shuttle landing on any boundary line of the proper court is still in play.
4. A shuttle landing outside the proper court area is out, even if the opponent had swung and missed the shuttle completely.
5. After the serve is completed, players on either side may take any position they wish irrespective of boundaries.
6. A shuttle cannot strike the roof, side walls, or touch any person (whether or not a player), or the person's clothes.
7. A player cannot touch the net or net posts with his body, racket, or his clothing, when the shuttle is in play.
8. A player must contact the shuttle on his side of the net; only on the follow-through of a stroke may a player's racket pass on the opponent's side of the court, provided he does not touch the net.
9. A player cannot step on his opponent's side of the net.
10. A player cannot "carry" the bird.
11. The shuttle may not be hit twice in succession before being returned to the opponent.

Lets

The following are deemed lets, as they result in a replaying of the point.

1. A let can occur if a stray shuttle or other object from a nearby court interferes with a player.
2. A let can occur if a decision on a particular shot cannot be made.
3. Sometimes where there is a low ceiling, the local association may establish a preliminary ground rule that this occurrence is a let. However if the obstruction can be deliberately hit, the fault rule is usually enforced.
4. It is a let if a serve is made before the receiver is ready; if the receiver returns the shuttle, however, it is assumed that he was ready.

BIBLIOGRAPHY

Books

Davidson, Kenneth, and Lealand Gustavson. *Winning Badminton.* New York: The Ronald Press Co., 1953.

Friedrich, John, and Abbie Rutledge. *Beginning Badminton.* Belmont, California: Wadsworth Publishing Company, Inc., 1962.

Grant, Doug. *Badminton.* Montreal: Graphic Publishing Co., 1950.

Varner, Margaret. *Badminton.* Dubuque, Iowa: Wm. C. Brown Company Publishers, 1966.

Articles

Miller, Frances A. "A Badminton Wall Volley Test," *Research Quarterly,* 22(2):208-215, May, 1951.

Thorpe, JoAnne. "Intelligence and Skill in Relation to Success in Singles Competition in Badminton and Tennis," *Research Quarterly,* 38(1):119-125, March, 1967.

Young, Olive G. "Rate of Learning in Relation to Spacing of Practice Periods in Archery and Badminton," *Research Quarterly,* 25(2):231-243, May, 1954.

CHAPTER

3

BOWLING

BEHAVIORAL OBJECTIVES

1. Given a bowling ball, the college student will be able to successfully demonstrate (meet *all* of the essential criteria as specified in the chapter) the following bowling fundamentals:
   a. Stance.
   b. Straight Delivery Grip.
   c. Hook Delivery Grip.
   d. Back-Up Delivery Grip.
   e. Four-Step Approach.
   f. Straight Delivery.
   g. Hook Delivery.
   h. Back-Up Delivery.
   i. Release.
   j. Follow-Through.
2. The college student will be able to demonstrate cross-lane spare bowling by converting the following spare leaves: 7-pin; 10-pin; 5-pin; 2-7 (Baby Split); 1-3-6-10 (Fence); and 1-2-4-10 (Washout).
3. The college student will be able to achieve a score of at least 75 per cent on a written examination concerned with the history, scoring, terminology and analysis of bowling fundamentals.

HISTORY OF BOWLING

The modern American game of bowling comes from an early religious ceremony that existed in Germany at the start of the Christian era. At that time, a club called a Kegel, was carried by all Germans. These were used for weapons, recreation, and religious purposes. A religious custom called upon the German to stand his Kegel at the end of a long runway. If a rolled stone hit his Kegel, which was referred to as Heide (heathen), he was living an honorable life. If he missed, he had to return until he succeeded in abolishing Heide. This custom was discontinued during the Dark Ages, but the monks began to set up all of their Kegels together, and to throw to see how many could be knocked down with a single roll. This recreational activity soon became popular throughout Germany. Martin Luther published a set of standardized rules and established the game of nine pins. The game spread throughout Europe, taking many forms. The Dutch brought bowling to America, and the first lanes were set up in New Amsterdam in 1623. By 1840, bowling had become the most popular game in New York. As has been true in many sports, gambling became prevalent, and bowling was outlawed in some states. An ingenious American added the tenth pin, thus circumventing the law against nine pins.

In 1895 the American Bowling Congress came into being. Alleys, equipment, and rules were standardized. Since that time bowling has spread through the very fabric of American life. Today it ranks high on the list of recreational activities.

NATURE OF BOWLING

Each bowler tries to knock down as many pins as possible with each ball rolled. (See Figure 3-1) Each bowler is allowed to roll two balls consecutively in each of the ten frames that constitute a game. If all ten pins are knocked down with the first ball a strike is awarded and the second ball is not needed. If two balls are needed to knock down all the pins, a spare is awarded, followed by a respotting of the pins for the next bowler. The player with the highest score after ten frames is the winner. The highest obtainable score in bowling is 300.

Bowling is the ideal sport for students, families, boys and girls. A beginner can start knocking down pins the first try, and a fair measure of success can be achieved quickly. Co-recreational bowling has become very popular. Many college students participate because of the social opportunities incorporated into the game. Thousands of leagues, for both sexes and all ages, are scheduled throughout the nation. Bowling truly is a sport for all.

EQUIPMENT

The Ball and Shoes

The ball is the most important item of equipment and should be selected with care. The selecting of a ball that fits properly is simple if certain principles are followed. The span (distance between thumb and finger holes) is more important than weight. When the span is too wide, the muscles of the hand become strained and tired; if too narrow, the fingers are pinched and the ball may be released prematurely. To determine the proper span, insert the thumb about three-quarters of its length into the proper hole, and extend the middle and ring finger across the finger holes. The middle knuckles of each finger should extend slightly over the holes. Alley balls are generally found with the conventional grips; but an individual may purchase a ball in which span, pitch of the holes, and size of the holes are fitted to his hand. (See Figure 3-2)

Figure 3-1. Ten Pin Set-Up.

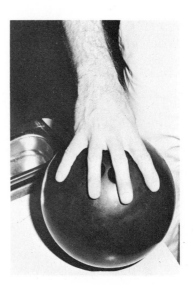

Figure 3-2. Correct Ball Fit.

Ball weights range from 10 to 16 pounds. Most men prefer a ball in the 13 to 16 pound class, while it is recommended that a woman use a 12 to 15 pound ball. One should try to use the heaviest ball possible if no noticeable difference is made in delivery.

Ball carriers are made to protect the ball from damage during transportation. Carriers should be kept clean of dirt and grit.

Bowling shoes are recommended and can be rented at the alley. Under no circumstances should bowling shoes be worn outdoors or be allowed to get wet.

SKILLS TO BE DEVELOPED

Excellence in bowling comes about from a combination of physical skill and mental discipline. Many beginners completely disregard the period prior to delivery. This should be the time to take a careful look at the pins; to make a mental check of the ensuing approach and release; and to build confidence that the delivery will be successful. A bowler's competitive spirit is intangeable. However, the success of past performances will put the individual in the correct frame of mind. The pre-delivery period should be accentuated by a singleness of purpose; i.e., to knock down as many pins as possible.

The entire procedure of approach, delivery, and follow-through should be smooth and relaxed. To accomplish this, certain skills must be developed.

Stance

The distance from the foul line at which the bowler stands to address the pins depends upon the number and length of steps. The position, in relation to left, center, and right sides of the lane, depends on the type of delivery. The straight-ball bowler will assume a position to the right of center if he is right handed. His ball will travel right to left. The curve-ball delivery will necessitate a stance left of center, so that the ball will roll right then left into the pins. When addressing the pins, the feet should be close together with one foot slightly ahead of the other. As the bowler becomes more experienced, individual foot variations may be made. The body is erect with the shoulders squarely facing the pins. The ball should be held at waist level and slightly to the right center side of the body. (See Figure 3-3)

Grip (Straight Delivery)

The ball is supported by the non-bowling hand. The fingers of the bowling hand should be under the ball so that the palm is supinated (facing upward). The thumb is pointed to a twelve o'clock position.

Approach

When outstanding bowlers are observed, it is noted that there are many similarities in the approach. The single objective being a release just short of the foul line. To become proficient, a person must be able to do exactly the same thing in the same way with every

Figure 3-3. Proper Stance.

delivery. He must be consistent in everything he does. A spot on the
approach (twelve to fifteen feet from the foul line) should be selected before movement to the foul line is started. This spot should
remain constant on all lanes. As experience is gained, individual variations may be made, but a beginner needs a definite spot from which
to work.

The bowler may take three, four, or more steps in making his
approach. He must select the approach which will allow the ball and
left foot to reach a spot just short of the foul line simultaneously.
Most beginners should start with the four-step approach because of
its simplicity. On the first step, a short one, the ball is pushed forward from the body towards the pins. On the second step, somewhat
larger, the ball swings downward and passes by the body. On the
third step, the ball reaches the top of the backswing, roughly $180°$
from the starting position and starts downward. On the fourth step, a
slide step, the ball passes by the body and is released on the lane
beyond the foul line. The feet remain close to the floor throughout
the first three steps and the knees are slightly bent, while in the
fourth step the left knee is well bent. (See Figure 3-4)

Figure 3-4. Four Step Approach.

Release

The release is the moment the ball leaves the hand. This is the most critical movement in bowling. The ball should be released just beyond the foul line. The ball hand must then follow through on a straight line with the palm facing skyward. (See Figure 3-5) A rolling of the wrist either clockwise or counter-clockwise will cause the ball to deviate from the straight line.

Figure 3-5. Release.

Hook, Curve and Back-Up Deliveries

The hook, curve and back-up deliveries deviate from the straight line delivery. The hook and curve balls are desirable because they increase the angle and amount of spin upon hitting the pins, thus picking up more wood and increasing scores. It is recommended that only those who have mastered the straight ball delivery attempt to use another method because the hook and curve balls add additional variables to the game.

Hook Ball Delivery. The hook ball is delivered by holding your thumb in the 10 o'clock position. This places the fingers at 4 o'clock. The wrist is rigid. As you release your thumb, the fingers life counterclockwise and up toward the ceiling in order to impart the necessary spin.

Curve Ball Delivery. The curve ball is an exaggerated hook. This type of delivery is very difficult to control. The grip is the same as that used for the hook, but the ball is released closer to the center of the lane and travels slowly toward the pins describing a wide arc.

Back-Up Delivery. The ball is held in a manner similar to that used for a straight ball delivery. As the ball is released, the hand rotates outward imparting a clockwise spin on the ball. (See Figure 3-6)

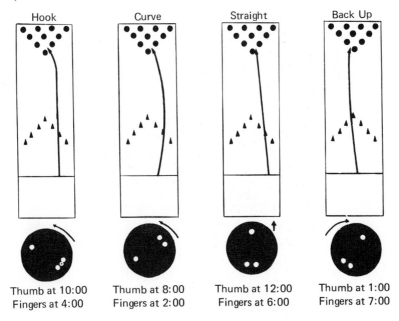

Figure 3-6. Four Types of Delivery.

Speed

Bowling is a game of accuracy, not speed. Ball speed is dependent on the approach and arm swing; accuracy should not be sacrificed for speed. Many times the pins are hit with such force that they leave the lane vertically, thus reducing the possibility of hitting one another.

Aiming

The two major methods of aiming are pin and spot. Most good bowlers use the spot method.

Pin Aiming. Pin aiming is recommended for beginners because it is natural to aim by concentrating exactly on the pins expected to be hit.

Spot Aiming. The spot bowler using this method plots an imaginary line along the path the ball is expected to travel. A spot on that line is selected, usually about fifteen feet out from the foul line. This spot becomes the focal point during the approach and delivery. With practice a bowler will determine spots for spare leaves as well as for full setups. (See Figure 3-7)

Right-handed bowlers whether delivering a straight, hook, or curve ball should try to strike the pins in the 1-3 pocket, being certain to carry the five pin solidly. The one, two, four, and seven pins are carried by each other. The three pin carries the six which carries the ten. The five pin carries the eight pin as the ball travels to the back line to the nine pin. If the five pin remains standing after a pocket hit, the hit was probably too *thin*. (See Figure 3-8)

Figure 3-7. Spots for Aiming.

Figure 3-8. One-Three Pocket.

Spare Leaves

There are many possible combinations of spare leaves, and a bowler who expects high scores must be particularly adept in picking up these pins. The following are general recommendations for picking up spare leaves:

1. When spare leaves remain on the left of center (2-4-5-7-8), the strike shot approach position is recommended. Adjustment to the remaining pins or moving of the spot will be necessary. (See Figure 3-9)

2. When spare leaves remain on the right of center (6-9-10), a position left of center on the approach is recommended. Adjustment to the remaining pins or moving of the spot will be necessary. (See Figure 3-9)

3. The technique illustrated in A and B is called cross-alley spare bowling. Emphasis is put on using as much alley as possible in making spares when using this technique.

4. When pins are left in the middle of the lane (1-3), use the strike delivery.

5. Single pin leaves should be hit dead-center.

a.   b.

Figure 3-9. Cross Alley Spare Bowling.

6. When one pin is directly behind another, the front pin must be hit on the nose.

7. When three or more pins are clustered together, aim for the middle pin.

8. Spare bowling is the key to high scores, "Good bowlers are spare bowlers."

Splits

Splits are difficult because of the space between pins. The frequency of converting splits to spares depends on the distance between pins.

1. To pick up the baby split (3-10 or 2-7) roll across alley, hitting the front pin on the outside so that it knocks down rear pin.

2. When two pins stand side by side, such as the 4-5 split, aim directly at the opening between the pins.

3. To pick up the 5-7 or 5-10 split aim to the outside of the 5 pin to deflect it into the remaining pin.

4. As splits get more difficult, 4-6-7-10 or 7-10, it is recommended that a try for the easiest of the two pins be attempted.

Scoring

Scoring is cumulative, i.e., to the total of each frame is added the sum of the pins knocked down in the next frame plus bonuses for strikes or spares, if any.

1. A strike scores ten pins plus the total pins knocked down with the next two balls. An "X" is recorded in the first box in the upper right-hand corner.

2. A spare scores ten pins plus the total pins knocked down with the next ball. A "/" is recorded in the first box in the upper right hand corner.

3. If a bowler strikes in the tenth frame, two additional balls are rolled before the score can be awarded for that frame.

4. If a bowler spares in the tenth frame, one additional ball is rolled before the score can be awarded for that frame.

5. An error, miss, or *blow* occurs if a spare is not made on the second ball. An error is recorded as a (—) in the box in the upper right-hand corner. Missing a split leave does not constitute an error or *blow*.

6. A split occurs if one pin is knocked down by the first ball and at least one pin is down between any two remaining pins. A split is designated by an "O" placed in the box in the upper right-hand corner.

7. A gutter ball is indicated by a "G" in the appropriate box of the frame.

8. A foul is indicated by a "F" in the appropriate box of the frame.

Etiquette

Etiquette rules are devised to add to the game. Safety, convenience, and respect for others are the major considerations. There are a few rules to be considered during the game:

1. Be ready to bowl when it is your turn.
2. Do not distract a bowler once he has taken his address position.
3. Stay behind the vision of the bowler preparing to bowl on the immediate left or right.
4. Stand off of the approach while waiting for your ball to be returned.
5. Do not loft or drop the ball.
6. The bowler on the right always goes first when adjacent alleys are ready at the same time.
7. Do not bait or upset your opponent by noise or gestures.
8. Do not take food or beverage onto the approach area.
9. Stay in your approach area at all times.
10. Wait until all pins are reset before address.
11. Always return balls to the proper storage racks.
12. Always use your own ball.
13. Hazardous approach conditions should be reported to the manager.
14. Do not complain.

Common Problems and Suggested Corrections

Problems	Corrections
1. Dropping ball behind foul line	Try lighter ball; try ball with wider span; slow approach; keep shoulder square at release.
2. Lofting ball	Try ball with larger finger holes; hold ball lower in stance; reduce backswing.
3. Bowling a back-up ball	Keep wrist stiff throughout delivery; keep thumb pointed towards pins.

4. Lack of speed	Increase backswing; increase approach speed.
5. Excess speed	Try heavier ball; reduce backswing; shorten approach steps.
6. Unbalanced release	Bend knee at release; keep shoulders square to pins; shorten approach steps; keep toe pointing forward.
7. Poor pin action	Increase angle to pins; increase ball speed; follow through at release.
8. Fouling with foot	Decrease size of approach steps; shorten first step of approach.
9. Guttering the ball	Approach pins in a straight line; keep shoulders square to pins; keep wrist stiff throughout delivery; examine angle to pins.
10. Tired arm and hand	Reduce span of ball, may be improper fit; keep swing natural without forcing release.
11. Hooking or curving ball	Keep wrist stiff throughout delivery; examine position of thumb at release.
12. Inaccurate delivery	Concentrate on the ensuing shot; keep swing vertical.

SIMPLIFIED RULES

1. It is a foul if, during the delivery, any part of the body or any implement carried on the body comes in contact with the foul line or any part of the lane. If a foul occurs on the first ball of a frame, the pins must be reset and the pin count is not allowed. The bowler then has one ball remaining in the frame. If he should knock down all ten pins a spare is awarded. If a foul occurs on the second ball, only the pins knocked down with the first ball are counted.

2. Pinfall is not allowed if the ball leaves the lane and then rebounds to knock down pins.

3. Pinfall is not allowed if knocked down by the pin setter. Mechanical pinfalls must be reported to the manager of the lanes for respotting.

TERMINOLOGY

Anchor—The last bowler on the team, usually the highest average.

Approach—The part of the alley extending back 15 ft. from the foul line.

Baby Split—The 2-7 and 3-10.

Back-up—A ball that fades to the bowler's right as it travels down the alley.

Bedposts—The 7-10 split.

Big Four—The 4-6-7-10 split.

Blow—Failure to convert a spare, other than a split.

Bucket—The 2-4-5-8 leave or 3-5-6-9 leave.

Chop—Chopping off the front pin or pins of a spare leave.

Clothes Line—The 1-2-4-7 or 1-3-6-10.

Curve—A ball that travels to the pins in a wide arc.

Dead Wood—Pins that have been knocked down.

Double—Two consecutive strikes.

Dutch 200—A game in which strikes and spares, or spares and strikes alternate throughout.

Foul—The act of touching beyond the foul line.

Frame—One-tenth of a game.

Full Hit—A ball that hits the center of a pin.

Gutter—Rounded areas on each side of the lane.

Handicap—A predetermined number of pins given in competition to a low average bowler or team.

Head Pin—The number one pin.

Kegler—A bowler.

King Pin—The number five pin.

Lane—Alley.

Leave—Pins standing after the first ball of a frame has been rolled.

Line—Game.

Loft—To release the ball high above the lane.

Mark—Making a strike or spare in a frame.

Open Frame—A frame without a strike or spare.

Perfect Game—Twelve consecutive strikes, a score of 300.

Pitch—Angle of finger holes in a ball.

Pocket—Space between the 1-3 pins for right-handed bowlers; between the 1-2 pins for the left-handed bowler.

Scratch—Using earned scores without a handicap.

Series—Three games.

Sleeper—The rear pin of a two-pin leave, in which the rear pin is not clearly visible.

Span—The distance between the finger and thumb holes on a bowling
ball.

Spare—Knocking down all ten pins with two consecutive balls.

Split—A leave in which the head pin is down and space remains
between the remaining pins.

Spot—Spots on the lane used for aiming.

Tap—A pin left after an apparently perfect hit, usually the eight or
ten pin.

Thin Hit—A less than center hit of a pin.

Turkey—Three consecutive strikes.

Washout—Split with the head pin standing (not a true split).

BIBLIOGRAPHY

Day, Ned. *How to Bowl Better*. New York: Arco Publishing Co., 1960.

Falcaro, J., and M. Goodman. *Bowling for All*. New York: The Ronald Press Co.,
1957.

McMahon, Junie, and M. Goodman. *Modern Bowling Techniques*. New York:
The Ronald Press Co., 1958.

Wilman, Joe. *Better Bowling*. New York: The Ronald Press Co., 1953.

CHAPTER

4

CANOEING

BEHAVIORAL OBJECTIVES

1. Given a 16-foot canoe and paddle, the college student will be able to successfully demonstrate (meet *all* of the essential criteria as specified in the chapter) the following canoeing fundamentals:
   a. Carrying.
   b. Launching.
   c. Boarding.
   d. Disembarking.
   e. Bow Stroke.
   f. Backwater Stroke.
   g. Draw Stroke.
   h. Pushover Stroke.
   i. Forward Sweep.
   j. Reverse Sweep.
   k. Bow Rudder.
   l. Crossbow Rudder.
   m. J-Stroke.
2. Given a 16-foot canoe, paddle, kneeling pad and life preserver, the college student will be able to keep a canoe on a straight course for 50 yards.
3. In still water, after taking ten successive strokes, the college student will be able to safely stop the canoe within a five-second time period.
4. Under normal water conditions, the college student will be able to bring the canoe toward the dock moving sideways for a distance of 10 yards.
5. Under normal water conditions, the college student will be able to maneuver the canoe in a figure-eight course within a 20-yard area.
6. Under normal water conditions, the college student will be able to execute a 360 degree pivot turn.

7. The college student will be able to achieve a score of at least 75 per cent on a written examination concerned with the history, terminology, canoeing safety and analysis of canoeing fundamentals.

HISTORY OF CANOEING

Historians tell us that civilization owes much of its success to water transportation. It is believed that the small boats of earliest man were the forerunners of our modern canoes. As man developed his skills and talents, he made use of certain objects in his struggle to survive. Those who lived near water developed the *dugout* for just such a purpose. The earliest crafts were usually made from a large tree, burnt and dug out to a point where they were large enough to accommodate passengers. These early dugouts were used for trading, transportation, recreation and warfare in most parts of the world. As might be expected, some primitive tribes still use these vessels as their principal form of transportation.

While these early crafts are not considered striking compared to our present standards, each was unique and useful to its time. They varied in size and capacity, from vessels designed to carry a single person to those capable of supporting large numbers of persons. The type of craft varied according to the locale. The Eskimo kayak, for example, was made of sealskin with a covered deck to give protection against the severe cold of the Arctic. Outrigger dugout canoes, such as the type found among the many islands of the Pacific Ocean, had cloth canopies which protected the occupant from the tropical sun.

The word *canoe* is an Indian term—*Arawakan* in origin. It was originally spelled *canoa*. The term was carried back to Europe by the early explorers and eventually was Anglicized as *canoe*. It was the birchbark canoe, developed primarily by the Indians of North America, that serves as the model for today's craft.

Twentieth Century canoeing has been expanded beyond the role of basic transportation. Canoeing is now incorporated into many summer camp recreational programs. While many sports-minded individuals use the canoe for hunting and fishing trips, others prefer White Water Canoeing, racing and kayaking. Also, a variety of canoes are used by those interested in competition. Canoeing is international in scope and is a regular event in the Summer Olympic Games.

NATURE OF CANOEING

The esthetic value of canoeing is often overlooked in lists of course objectives for the activity. Everyone should experience the exhilaration of paddling a canoe on a peaceful lake or stream on a cool autumn day. With man's renewed interest in ecology, what better place to feel close to nature?

The purpose of this chapter will be to explain the fundamentals of canoeing, so as to allow the reader to participate on a recreational skill level rather than on a competitive basis. Skills will be developed enabling the student to paddle a canoe on both sides with equal skill and safety. This permits necessary flexibility in adjusting to varied situations which may occur. There are several reasons why co-ed, tandem paddling is recommended as the most satisfactory method for beginners: (a) safety-assistance is close; (b) easier to master techniques; (c) better utilization of equipment; (d) stronger paddler helps weaker one. At all times, safety must be stressed. If the potential canoeist does not know how to swim, he *must* wear a special life preserver. Flotation devices *must* be supplied to all participants.

EQUIPMENT

Canoes

Canoes are available in many shapes and sizes. The type selected by the canoeist will be determined by the amount of the load to be carried, the purpose for which it is to be used, as well as the type of water in which it will be used. It is wise for the beginner to consult with the experienced person or reputable dealer for advice on this matter. Additional factors to consider, other than initial cost, are upkeep, design, weight, length, durability, and ease of repair.

For recreational purposes and all-around performance, the 16-foot canoe is usually the one recommended. This type has proven successful in the teaching of canoeing at the college level. (See Figure 4-1)

Canvas-covered and wooden canoes are still in use today; however, aluminum, fiber glass, plastic and rubber are becoming increasingly popular.

Paddles

Paddles also are made in many shapes and sizes. Selection depends upon the canoeist's experience, and on natural and local condi-

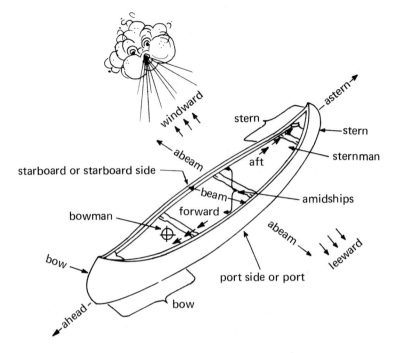

Figure 4-1. Canoe Parts and Terminology.

tions. One may choose from a wide variety of woods such as ash, maple, cherry, spruce, cedar, pine, fir, and basswood. Spruce paddles are frequently used because they are light in weight and easily handled by beginners. The better single-blade paddle is constructed in sections. This arrangement gives added strength over the paddle which is made of a single piece of wood (generally mass produced). A hardwood paddle, such as ash, generally is better able to withstand the hard use that a beginner tends to give it. The individual will eventually determine, through experience, the paddle which feels right and works best for him. (See Figure 4-2)

The proper paddle length is usually one that measures somewhere between the chin and nose when placed upright in front of the canoeist.

Double-blade paddles are sometimes used for solo cruising. This type is usually joined at the center by a ferrule joint which enables the blades to be set at right angles to each other. The length ranges between 9 and 10 feet.

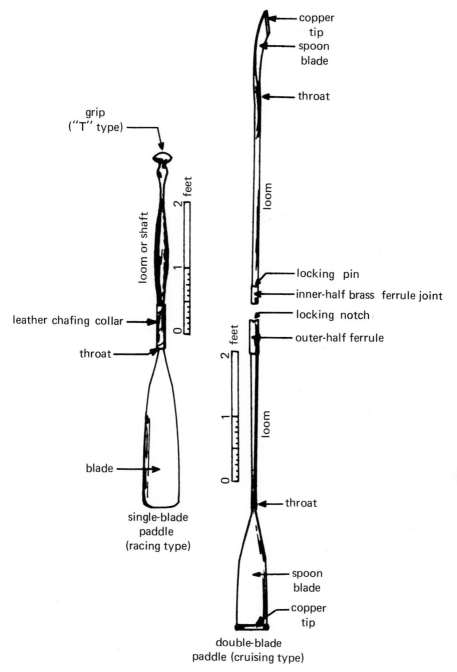

Figure 4-2. Paddle and Parts.

Accessory Equipment

Kneeling Pad. Since many people find it uncomfortable to kneel for extended periods of time in a canoe (kneeling adds to stability, and is the recommended paddling position), pads are used for the canoeist's comfort. Rubber pads, sponge knee pads, old sneakers, rolled-up towels, hot water bottles filled with cloth, and life preserver cushions are used for this purpose. In instructional situations, life preserver cushions are advisable in that they serve a dual purpose.

Life Jackets. For trips into unknown or rough waters, United States Coast Guard life jackets are recommended. This type of life

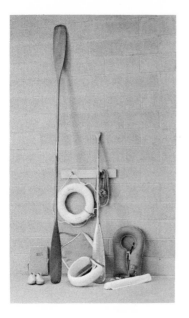

jacket is a necessity for all non-swimmers and poor swimmers. The swimming level of each student should be determined before anyone enters a canoe.

Tie Line. A tie line is used to secure the canoe to the dock, beach or bank.

Extra Paddle. For added safety, an extra paddle should always be carried on board. (See Figure 4-3)

SKILLS TO BE DEVELOPED

Carrying

Depending on the distance the canoe must be carried from the land to the water's edge, the craft may be carried in a number of ways. Although it is possible for one person to carry a canoe a short

Figure 4-3. Accessory Equipment.

distance, it is usually not recommended. The writer, therefore, shall describe only the two-man carry which is the most practical in the college class situation.

One person is positioned at each end of the canoe. The canoe is right-side up as it would be if it were floating normally in the water. The person at the bow has his hand inverted, his arm is in the palm out position, and his elbow is away from the body. The canoe is lifted and support is given under the keel. The person at the stern is on the same side and has reached around the canoe with his hand also under the keel. The sternman, however, does not have to rotate his hand. The stern of the canoe is wedged between the body and the arm. This keeps the canoe from rolling out of the bowman's hand. (See Figure 4-4)

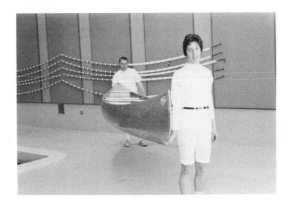

Figure 4-4. Two-Man Carry.

Launching

Again, the writer will describe only the two-man launching technique since it has proven the most successful in the teaching situation.

From a dock, the partners move to the center of the canoe on opposite sides facing one another. The canoe is held at right angles to the front edge of the dock. The hands are spread shoulder distance apart, gripping the gunwales. The knees are slightly bent. Lifting the canoe by the gunwales, it is fed out hand-over-hand into the water. Care should be given to avoid scraping the keel along the dock as this may cause damage. One person can now hold onto the canoe and bring it around parallel with the dock while the other partner returns for the paddles and accessory equipment. (See Figure 4-5)

For launching a canoe from the beach, the same technique is used with the exception that the canoe is not fed out all the way into the water, and is kept at right angles to the beach. Then the paddles and accessory equipment are placed into the canoe. Be sure to take along that extra paddle! (See Figure 4-6)

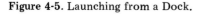

Figure 4-5. Launching from a Dock.

Figure 4-6. Launching from the Beach.

Boarding and Disembarking

Entering a canoe from the dock is not a difficult maneuver providing one follows a few basic rules:

1. Move the canoe so that it is alongside and parallel to the dock—being held in position by your partner.
2. When entering the canoe, keep your weight low and centered over the keel. Transfer your weight from your foot on the dock to the one in the canoe.
3. Look ahead in the canoe and enter at a point near amidship.
4. Move slowly, sliding hands along gunwales and keeping weight low toward the paddling position until paddling position has been reached.
5. The sternman enters the canoe first and backs into proper paddling position. (See Figure 4-7)

Entering a canoe from the beach is a little more difficult than from the dock, and requires more practice. The canoe is held at right angles to the shore line; the end nearest the shore is barely touching bottom. The sternman braces the canoe between his knees and hands while the bowman steps directly over the keel into the canoe. Keeping his center of gravity low and centered over the keel, the bowman grasps the gunwales on both sides and moves forward slowly and carefully. Upon reaching the paddling position, he kneels and gets his paddle (which had been placed on the bottom of the canoe). The sternman, who is still on shore, pushes the canoe away from the beach now to avoid grounding it. He puts one foot into the canoe, grasping both gunwales, then uses his rear foot (the one still on land) as a push device much as a child uses his leg on a scooter. (See Figure 4-8)

a.   b.

c.

Figure 4-7. Boarding from a Dock.

Figure 4-8. Boarding from the Beach.

For unloading from the dock as well as the beach, the order of events is reversed. When unloading on the beach, it is usually more convenient to come into shore bow first.

Paddling Position

For reasons of safety, the beginning canoeist should assume a relatively low paddling position in the canoe. There are two recommended positions:

Kneeling. The paddler kneels on the bottom of the canoe with his seat resting against the thwart (brace). This position keeps the weight low and over the keel. For comfort, a kneeling pad is recommended when the paddler will be kneeling for extended periods of time. For relief from the standard kneeling position, the knee opposite the paddling side may be raised with the foot and leg braced against the side of the canoe.

Sitting on the heels. The paddler kneels on the bottom of the canoe and then rests back on the inside part of the heel. This method is more difficult than the kneeling position to master for extended periods of time; however, the canoeist is very low, and this makes for a stable craft.

Paddling Skills

Tandem paddling is always done on opposite sides of the canoe with periodic changes from side to side made to reduce fatigue. It is essential that both partners communicate with each other to allow for efficient operation. Usually, the sternman is in command of the vessel, while it is the bowman's responsibility to watch for obstructions. In the tandem situation, the sternman takes his place in front of the stern seat or thwart and the bowman takes his place in front of the bow seat or thwart. Both are in the kneeling position. Tandem paddling works most efficiently when both paddlers are about evenly matched in power; however, this is not always possible and adjustments must be made while paddling. If given a choice, usually the stronger paddler should be in the stern.

Paddling Strokes

The proper position of the hands on the paddle is basically the same for all strokes explained in this chapter. The paddle is held so that the lower hand is placed nearest the paddling side around the loam just above the flair of the blade. The hand should be kept just above the water level so as to allow for good leverage without getting wet. The top hand grips the paddle at the grip, knuckles on the top and the thumb pointed outward. The top hand grasps the grip firmly, the lower hand holds the loam loosely to allow the blade to be twisted right or left as necessary to carry out a particular stroke.

The Bow Stroke

This is the basic stroke upon which most of the other strokes are built. It is the stroke which gives the canoe forward movement.

To begin the stroke, the paddle is reached forward with the top hand just out beyond the chin, the top arm is extended forward. The paddle is dipped, pulling it parallel to the side of the canoe with the top arm and pushing away from the chin with the other arm. By exerting an equal push-pull action, power will be exerted by the blade as it moves through the water. When the paddle blade has passed the hip, lift it from the water. You are ready to repeat the stroke. A good paddling rhythm is necessary in order to achieve smooth propulsion. The bowman usually sets the pace. (See Figure 4-9)

a.   b.

c.

Figure 4-9. Bow Stroke.

The Backwater Stroke

This stroke is used to stop the canoe or to make it move into reverse. The canoeist dips the paddle behind him and exerts forward pressure with the lower arm. The stroke starts where the bow stroke ends, and is actually the reverse of that stroke. (See Figure 4-10)

Figure 4-10. Backwater Stroke.

The Draw Stroke

This stroke is sometimes used to move the canoe sideward toward the paddling side. It is executed by reaching well out (about twenty inches) at right angles to the side of the craft, and drawing the flat side of the blade toward the paddler. This moves the canoe sideward toward the point from which the stroke was made. Both bowman and sternman find this stroke useful for changing direction or approaching the dock for a landing.

The recovery for the draw stroke can be made on top of or under the water by turning the blade 90° at the completion of the stroke and then slicing it back through the water to the starting point. (See Figure 4-11)

The Pushover Stroke

Sometimes called the Pushaway Stroke, this stroke is used to move the canoe sideways—away from the paddling side. The paddle is used to thrust or pry the craft from a given point. The paddle blade is first inserted straight down and slightly under the canoe with the flat surface facing the side of the canoe. The top hand should be way out over the water. A pushing action with the hand on the throat of the paddle, and a pulling down action with the top hand is

Figure 4-11. The Draw Stroke.

necessary. Equal pressure should be exerted with both hands during the stroke to achieve the best results.

An under or over the water recovery may be employed. In the underwater recovery, the blade action will be the reverse of the one employed for the draw stroke. The pushover is really the reverse of the draw stroke.

It is a useful stroke when moving the canoe into a good docking position. Both partners may use the pushover, or they can vary it by one using the draw stroke and the other using the pushover in order to move the canoe broadside. (See Figure 4-12)

Figure 4-12. The Pushover Stroke.

The Sweep Strokes

These strokes are used for partial or complete pivot turns. The paddle is extended horizontally to the side in line with the hip. The paddle is kept well extended with the hand on the grip at waist level and the flat portion of the blade facing forward. A horizontal sweeping motion is employed (by using the paddle as an oar) toward the stern. Good leverage may be employed by pulling with the bottom hand and pushing horizontally with the top hand. The tip of the paddle does a wide arc; usually the wider the sweep, the better. This stroke may be both forward, as the writer has described, or may be in reverse—in which case it is called a reverse sweep. For tandem paddlers, the sweep consists of a 90° arc. For single paddlers (located at amidships), a full 180° sweep is employed.

To allow the stationary canoe to complete a pivot turn, the bowman does a 90° forward sweep starting from the top of the canoe. At the same time, the sternman on the opposite side of the canoe does a 90° reverse sweep that starts from his end of the canoe. This action, if continued, will turn the canoe full circle. (See Figure 4-13)

a.

b.

Figure 4-13. The Sweep Stroke.

The "J" Stroke

The "J" stroke is considered a steering stroke. In tandem paddling, the sternman employs it to keep the canoe on course without losing any appreciable headway.

Basically, the stroke is the Bow stroke with certain modifications at the end. If the Bow stroke were used exclusively, the canoe would tend to move away from the paddling side and follow a crooked course down the stream. The J stroke is a smooth one-count stroke performed with the same timing and rhythm as its cousin, the Bow stroke. It differs from the bow stroke in that the paddle is turned and pulled through the water on an angle in the second half of the stroke. The inner edge of the paddle is backward with the blade parallel to the canoe. Both the canoeist's wrists are flexed to turn the blade face. The top grip hand, however, does the work in fixing the proper angle. To make the stroke easy and effective, the paddler should bear inward with his top hand so that the paddle shaft contacts the gunwale, causing the blade to exert pressure against the water thus forcing it away from the water. The thumb on the grip hand will be pointed downward and outward.

At the conclusion of the stroke, the return is made by slipping the paddle sideward out of the water, moving the blade ahead just off the surface of the water to the point where the next stroke may begin. (See Figure 4-14)

The Bow Rudder Stroke

This stroke moves the bow of the canoe sharply toward the bowman's paddling side. The bowman places the blade edgewise in

a.   b.

Figure 4-14. The "J" Stroke.

the water, close to the bow with the top edge slightly angled (20° to 30°) away from the bow. In this position, the flat part of the blade faces the canoe. The canoeist's hand nearest the shaft should remain low on the paddle to allow for contact with the gunwale (bracing and support). The top hand on the grip is braced against the shoulder with the elbow tight against the body or in line with the shaft. The bottom hand will have to slide up slightly on the shaft so that this hand can be braced against the gunwale. If executed properly, the paddle will act as a trap, and move the canoe in that direction.

Care should be taken not to extend the paddle too far out from the canoe as this will make it very difficult to hold the paddle in the desired position. (See Figure 4-15a)

The Cross-Bow Rudder Stroke

This stroke has the opposite effect to that of the Bow Rudder, and is done on the opposite paddling side. It is not necessary to change your grip on the paddle from the one just described for the Bow Rudder. The bowman swings the paddle across the bow and places the paddle in the water as for the Bow Rudder. The grip hand should be at waist level away from the body. The body must twist slightly and face that side of the canoe. The lower hand on the shaft is extended and is usually braced against the gunwale for better support. (See Figure 4-15b)

Although not a difficult stroke to master, it does take practice to perfect. The more rapidly the canoe is moving, the more strength is needed to hold the paddle in the desired position.

a.   b.

Figure 4-15. The Bow Rudder and Cross-Bow Rudder Strokes.

Double-Blade Paddling

This type of paddling can be done either by tandem or solo paddlers.

Double paddles are adjustable and the blades should be made to form right angles with each other. This allows one blade to be in the feathered position while the other is moving through the water. The hands are placed on the paddle slightly more than shoulder width apart.

Figure 4-16. Double-Blade Paddling.

To begin the stroke, the bottom arm is extended while the top arm is bent with the hand in front of the shoulder. The wrists should control the angle of the blade as it enters the water. The actual stroke is a pushing with the top arm as the bottom arm pulls. When the top arm is in the fully extended position, it is necessary to raise the hand at the hip to shoulder height while flipping the blade a 1/4 turn. This readies the paddle for the next stroke. (See Figure 4-16)

Canoe Safety

Water can be a dangerous place for recreational activities if safety rules are overlooked or treated lightly. A few common safety rules must be observed to make canoeing a safe activity for all involved.

1. A person should be able to swim in deep water, fully clothed, for a reasonable period of time.
2. Appropriate life preservers must be provided for each passenger. Non-swimmers must wear United States Coast Guard life jackets at all times.
3. Carry only the amount of weight the canoe was designed to carry.
4. A spare paddle should be on hand.
5. Keep the center of gravity low in the canoe. Do not shift your weight suddenly.
6. Wear suitable clothing that can be removed easily and safely in the water.
7. Check weather reports and be advised on unusual weather conditions. Never canoe in thunder storms.

8. Avoid night canoeing.

9. Keep near the shore as much as possible.

10. If you encounter rough waves and weather, it is important that you stay low, and keep one end of the canoe pointed toward the waves. In severe weather, lie down on the bottom and as near to the center as possible.

11. If it is necessary to change paddling positions, it should be done on dry land when at all possible.

12. Generally, it is wise to stay with a capsized or swamped canoe. It can be used as a life raft as it usually will not sink. An exception would be if the current were to carry the passenger toward rapids, rocks, waterfall, or some other water hazard.

13. Never endanger your safety in rescue work. Always try first to use equipment onboard the canoe. Extend a paddle to a tired swimmer rather than your arm.

14. White water canoeing requires experience, special skill and endurance. The beginner should seek expert advice.

15. Immature behavior and improper handling of equipment may lead to unnecessary injury.

16. Beginners should never take a canoe out alone. Practice under proper supervision.

17. Remember, common sense plays an important role in canoe safety.

18. Getting into a swamped canoe: Roll the canoe into the normal right-side-up position. Position yourself at amidship (generally has greatest stability). Gently reach inside and press down on the center with your hands. By kicking gently, level off. Hold on to the closest gunwale with one hand and reach for the far side thwart with the other hand. Moving slowly, pull your body, roll the hips, and sit on the bottom. Remember to move slowly as a swamped canoe is very unstable. A swamped canoe will usually support all its passengers safely. The passengers may paddle with their hands or resume regular paddling if paddles have not been lost.

TERMINOLOGY

Abeam—At right angles to the centerline of the canoe.
Aft—Toward the stern (rear).
Ahead—Ahead of the canoe.
Amidship—At the middle or center of the canoe.
Astern—Behind the canoe.

Beam—Point of greatest width of the canoe.

Blade—The large flat portion of the paddle which pulls through the water.

Bow—The extreme forward end of a canoe.

Bowman—Person who paddles in the forward portion of the canoe.

Deck—The portion of the canoe fitted between the gunwales at the extreme ends of the canoe.

Feather—Flat position of blade in recovery to reduce wind and water resistance.

Flare—The area of the paddle of increasing width where the shaft joins the blade.

Forward—Towards the bow.

Grip—The handle on top of the paddle at the opposite end to the blade.

Gunwale—The uppermost portion of the sides of the canoe extending around the canoe from bow to stern.

Keel—A strip on the outside bottom of the canoe in the centerline extending from bow to stern.

Keel Line—A center line on inside bottom of the canoe extending lengthwise from bow to stern.

Leeward—The side of the canoe or direction away from the wind.

Painter—Rope attached to bow or stern of the canoe (used in securing the canoe to shore).

Port—To the left side of the canoe.

Portage—To carry the canoe over land.

Ribs—Curved section of the canoe running crosswise from the keel to the gunwales.

Run—A stretch of fast, rough water.

Shaft—The long slender part of the paddle between the grip and the blade.

Starboard—To the right side of the canoe.

Stern—The rear portion of the canoe.

Sternman—Person who paddles in the rear position of the canoe.

Streamcraft—A sound knowledge of water movement and the ability to read the surface signs in the stream.

Throat—The junction of the shaft with the blade above the flare on the paddle.

Thwarts—Braces placed crosswise from gunwale to gunwale which help maintain canoe's shape.

Tip—The end of the paddle at the blade.

Trim—A canoe balanced evenly on keel by careful positioning of all weight within canoe.

Wake—Action of the water caused by the movement of the canoe.

White water—A stretch of fast moving, rough water sometimes obstructed by rocks above and below the surface.

Windward—The side of the canoe from which the wind is blowing.

BIBLIOGRAPHY

Adney, Edwin Tappan, and Howard I. Chapelle. *The Bark Canoes and Skin Boats of North America.* Washington, D.C.: Smithsonian Institution, 1964.

American Red Cross. *Canoeing.* Garden City, New York: Doubleday and Company, Inc., 1956.

Anderson, Luther A. *A Guide to Canoe Camping.* Chicago: Reilly and Lee, 1969.

Camp, Raymond R. *The Young Sportsman's Guide to Canoeing.* New York: Thomas Nelson and Sons, 1962.

Elvedt, Ruth. *Canoeing A-Z.* Minneapolis, Minnesota: Burgess Publishing Company, 1964.

Leslie, Robert Franklin. *Read the Wild Water.* New York: E.P. Dutton and Co., Inc., 1966.

Malo, John. *Malo's Complete Guide to Canoeing and Canoe-Camping.* Chicago: Quadrangle Books, 1969.

McNair, Robert E. *Basic River Canoeing.* Martinsville, Indiana: American Camping Association, Inc., 1969.

Perry, Ronald H. *Canoeing for Beginners.* New York: Associated Press, 1967.

Russell, Charles W. *Basic Canoeing.* The American National Red Cross, 1965.

Urban, John T. *A White Water Handbook for Canoe and Kayak.* Boston: Appalachian Mountain Club, 1965.

Vaughan, Linda Kent, and Richard Hale Stratton. *Canoeing and Sailing.* Dubuque, Iowa: William C. Brown Company Publishers, 1970.

FENCING

BEHAVIORAL OBJECTIVES

1. Given a French foil, under simulated bouting conditions, the college student will be able to successfully demonstrate (meet *all* of the essential criteria as specified in the chapter) the following foil fencing maneuvers:
   a. Grip.
   b. Attention Position.
   c. Salute.
   d. On-Guard Position.
   e. Advance.
   f. Retreat.
   g. Thrust.
   h. Lunge.
   i. Recovery Forward from Lunge.
   j. Recovery Backward from Lunge.
   k. Disengage.
   l. Cut-over.
   m. Beat.
   n. Parry Four.
   o. Parry Six.
   p. Parry Seven.
   q. Parry Eight.
2. The college student will be able to achieve a score of at least 75 per cent on a written examination concerned with the history, rules, terminology and analysis of fencing fundamentals.
3. The college student will be able to demonstrate successful competitive foil fencing ability by winning at least two out of four bouts in a round-robin class tournament composed of homogeneous groups of five fencers.

HISTORY OF FENCING

Some historians trace "sword-fighting" back past the Christian era. Ancient Greek, Roman and Persian soldiers are known to have used the sword as a major implement of war. Its mastery was an essential element of self-preservation during times of war. Originally, fencing required brute strength and a heavy sword rather than skillful footwork and finesse. During the sixteenth century, the rapier, a lighter and more graceful weapon, was introduced and eventually replaced the heavy sword. With the advent of firearms, the sword rapidly declined in value as a weapon of war. Yet, even in times of peace, the sword played an important function in settling affairs of honor and legal disputes.

Technique in the use of the sword began to develop as shorter, lighter court swords made possible many maneuvers that were not practical with the rapier. Fencing schools were established during the seventeenth century in France, Italy, and Spain. Swordsmanship then developed into a true sport in which the objective became to score points by a touch, and not to kill.

NATURE OF FENCING

The objective of the sport is to touch the opponent with the sword in such a fashion that a point is scored. Points are scored by making contact with the weapon. The first fencer scoring five touches (four touches needed in female bouts) is declared the winner with a ten-minute time limit for each bout. If a tie exists after the allotted time has elapsed, a "sudden death" procedure is employed in which the first fencer to score a touch is declared the winner.

Competition is conducted on a *piste* or strip approximately 40 feet long and 6 feet wide. (See Figure 5-1) To initiate a match, fencers face one another in an "on-guard" position and upon a given command, begin to fence. Action continues until the command

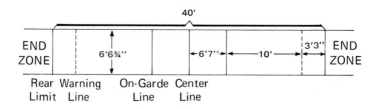

Figure 5-1. Fencing Piste.

"halt" is given by the President or Director of the bout. Once the validity of the touch has been determined by the judges, the fencers return to the on-guard position and resume action.

EQUIPMENT

Weapons

In the sport of fencing, there are three diversified weapons; the foil, the epee, and the sabre. The foil and epee are thrusting weapons while the sabre is used for both cutting and thrusting. Although a brief description of the epee and sabre are included, this section is mainly concerned with the element of foil fencing, because the foil is considered to be the most practical of the three weapons to teach in a college class situation.

The Epee. The epee or duelling sword, is heavier and less flexible than the foil. The blade of the epee is triangular and tapers from the base (forte) to a blunted tip. The target area includes the entire body. Valid touches must be made by the tip of the blade since the weapon is considered to be of the thrusting type.

The Sabre. The sabre, or old cavalry sword, is primarily a cutting weapon, although the point may be used. It has a triangular or T-shaped blade with a cutting edge along the length of the entire front and one-third of the back of the weapon. For maximum protection of the hand, the guard covers the entire length of the handle. The target area for sabre fencing consists of the arms, head and torso from the waist up.

The French Foil. The foil is the lightest of the three fencing weapons and is considered the basic weapon carried over from duelling practices. The blade is rectangular, and tapers from the forte through the flexible foible to the blunted tip. A metal guard is attached to protect the hand. Extending from the handle is the *pommel*, a weight used as a counter balance. (See Figure 5-2)

The head, arms and legs are considered *off-target* with the foil target area extending from the top of the collar to the groin lines in front, back and sides to a horizontal line passing across the top of the

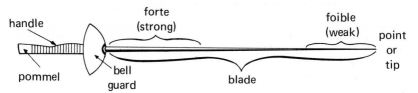

Figure 5-2. French Foil.

hip bones. A *touch*, or point is scored if the tip of the blade hits any part of the target area.

Mask

The mask protects a fencer's face and is always worn when facing an opponent. For maximum protection of face and neck, the mask has a wire mesh covering which protects the face and a bib attachment at the wire base to protect the throat. The tongue, which fits over the top and the back of the head, is used to adjust the mask to fit different sizes and shapes of heads.

Jacket

The jacket covers the arms and upper torso and should afford maximum protection to the entire target area. Most jackets are made of canvas material and should fit snuggly around the body. A "plastron," or half jacket, is a practice jacket which protects only the front and foil arm side of the body.

Glove

The glove or *gauntlet* is worn on the foil hand only to prevent minor cuts. To prohibit the opponent's blade from sliding up the jacket, the sleeve should always be tucked inside the glove as a safety precaution.

SKILLS TO BE DEVELOPED

The Grip

A foil with the French grip should be utilized in the instructional program. This type of grip enables beginning fencers to develop fine control of the blade and foil tip. When correctly held, the fingers can be effectively used to manipulate the foil. The grip is executed by placing the convex side of the handle diagonally in the palm at the heel of the thumb. (See Figure 5-3a) The thumb is placed on the broad surface of the handle close to the bell guard. The index finger is wrapped around the handle so that the foil rests between the first and second joints of the index finger. (See Figure 5-3b) The other three fingers should rest lightly along the left side of the handle. (See Figure 5-3c) The pommel should remain flush against the wrist so that the foil becomes an extension of the arm.

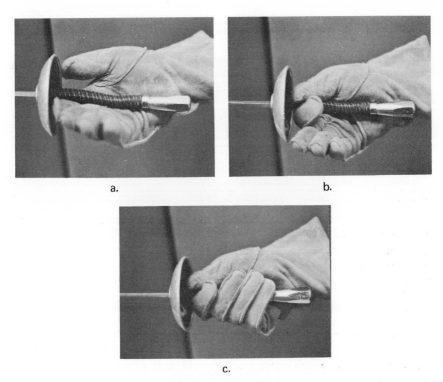

a.   b.

c.

Figure 5-3. The Grip.

Position of Attention

All fencers assume the position of attention while waiting for the command to fence or while the jury is deciding upon a phase of action during a bout. In this erect position, the feet are placed at right angles with the heels together. The front foot is pointed toward the opponent. The foil arm and foil are extended toward the floor over the front foot. The mask is held in the non-foil hand under the waist. The fencer's head is turned laterally so that he is looking over the foil arm directly at his opponent. (See Figure 5-4)

Salute

The traditional gesture of courtesy made to one's opponent, officials and audience prior to a bout and upon its completion is

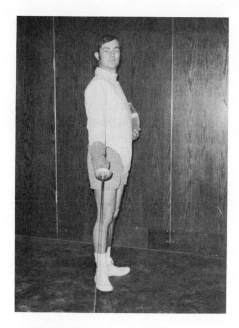

Figure 5-4. Position of Attention.

called the *salute*. It is executed from the position of attention. To
initiate the salute flex the foil arm at the elbow and raise the bell
guard to chin level. The palm of the foil hand is turned toward the
face and the foil is held straight up. (See Figure 5-5a) To complete
the salute, extend the foil arm shoulder high, with the point aiming
directly at your opponent's eyes. (See Figure 5-5b) Upon completing
these quick movements, the mask is put on with the non-foil hand.

On-Guard Position

A fencer moves into the on-guard position from the position of
attention. The on-guard position is the fundamental position of readiness for both offensive and defensive actions. In this position, the
feet are spaced a comfortable distance apart (approximately 18
inches) with the weight of the body equally distributed over this
wide base of support. The feet are at right angles with the heel of the
forward foot in front of the rear heel. With the feet positioned
properly, the fencer "sits down" bending his knees so that they are
positioned above the toes or instep of the positioned feet. The torso
is turned to offer a profile to the opponent. The foil arm is slightly

 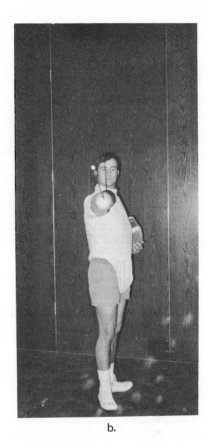

a.   b.

Figure 5-5. Salute.

flexed, with the elbow approximately six inches from the body. The palm is up with the hand held chest high. The non-foil arm is raised behind the head and held shoulder high. The elbow is flexed, forming a right angle with the upper arm, and the hand is flexed and relaxed hanging forward about head height. (See Figure 5-6) .

The Advance and Retreat

The basic foot movement from the guard position is that of the advance and the retreat. The advance is a movement which brings you closer to your opponent. It is executed without altering the on-guard position in any way. To advance, the front foot is lifted and moved ahead about 12 inches. As the heel touches the floor, the rear

Figure 5-6. On-Guard Position.

foot pushes off and moves forward the same distance so as to reassume the original spacing of the feet in the on-guard position.

The movement backward, or *retreat*, is employed in order to move away from an opponent or out of reach of a direct lunge by the opponent. To perform the retreat, the rear foot moves back about 12 inches and then the front foot is lifted and closed to the guard position. In both the advance and the retreat, fencers should avoid sliding the feet.

The Thrust and Lunge

The thrust is simply a quick extension of the foil arm with the intention of gaining a touch. This movement must precede the lunge in order that the ensuing action be considered legal. (See Right-of-Way Ruling) To execute the thrust, lower the point of the foil to the level of the target and then straighten the foil arm. As the tip strikes the target, the blade should bend upward. There should be no movement of the body or of the left arm.

The lunge is probably the fencer's most important offensive tactic, for it is the quickest method of closing the distance to an opponent. To perform the lunge, the foil arm is extended so that the guard is at shoulder height and the point of the foil is slightly lower than the foil of the floor as the rear leg is straightened. This action impels the body forward due to the explosive and forceful extension of the rear leg. The non-foil arm is flug backwards, palm up, to a position parallel to and directly over the rear leg. Once in the lunge position, the weight should be equally distributed between your base of support with your body in the following position: Forward knee bent directly over the instep of the forward foot; knee flexion beyond this point results in an overlunge and will hinder the recovery, or return to the on-guard position. Both feet are flat on the floor, with the front lower leg perpendicular to the floor. The rear leg and both arms fully extended with hips still under the trunk. (See Figure 5-7)

Figure 5-7. The Lunge.

The recovery from the lunge back to the guard position can be made either forward or backward. It enables a fencer to withdraw rapidly to a defensive position, or pursue the offensive attack after the lunge. To recover backward, the front foot pushes against the floor as the weight of the body is transferred to the rear leg. The rear knee and non-foil arm flex and return to the guard position.

If one's opponent has retreated out of range with the lunge attack, the fencer should recover forward. To recover forward, the rear leg is flexed and moved up to the guard position as the non-foil arm is quickly flexed at the elbow and also moved into the guard position.

Lines of Engagement

Theoretically, the fencing target is divided into four quadrants or lines. These four sections are classified into upper and lower lines as well as inside or outside lines. The bell guard divides the upper and lower lines while the foil arm delineates the inside and outside lines. Thus, there are four basic portions which must be protected: inside-high; inside-low; outside-high; and outside-low. (See Figure 5-8)

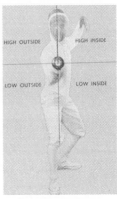

Figure 5-8. Lines of Engagement.

Blades are said to be engaged when the foibles of the two foils are in contact. Engagements are identified by number. When the opponent's blade is to the outside of your blade, you are engaged in sixth; when your opponent's blade is to the inside of yours, the engagement number is fourth. The low inside line is designated as seventh and the low-outside line as eighth.

Defensive Actions

Defensive actions which deflect attacking foils are called "parries." In order to move the opponent's blade out of line, a parry may be executed by sharply beating the opponent's blade or by applying continuous pressure. Parries are named according to the target sections which they protect.

Types of Parries

Simple or Direct Parries. Parries of this type are performed by rapidly shifting the on-guard position to the right or left and are designed to defend the high inside and outside lines. Thus, if a fencer is engaged in fourth, the sixth line will be open so an attack to this area would be defended by a direct parry six.

Semicircular Parries. A semicircular parry is an indirect parry performed by moving the foil from a high to a low line or from a low to a high line. The tip of the blade describes an arc as it moves to protect the target area.

Circular Parries. A circular or counter-parry is executed by moving the point in a circular fashion around the attacking blade and back to the original line of engagement. For example, in the counter-parry of sixth, the attacker attempts to shift his blade from the sixth to the fourth line. The defender drops his point under and around the threatening foil and carries it back to the original line of sixth.

Execution of Parries

Parry Four. This parry defends the high-inside line. As the wrist breaks laterally, the foil arm shifts to the left until it is in front of the left side of the body. The blade tip points just over the opponent's rear shoulder. In this position, the thumb should be on top of the handle.

Parry Six. This parry defends the high-outside line. The foil-hand moves to the right until the blade tip points over the opponent's left shoulder. The foil-hand rotates to the outside until the knuckles of the thumb are directly to the side and the pommel is brought in close to the wrist.

Parry Seven. This parry defends the low-inside line. To protect this area, the wrist of the foil-hand breaks downward as the tip moves clockwise to a position opposite the opponent's rear knee.

Parry Eight. This parry defends the low-outside line. The parry eight moves the foil downward in a counter-clockwise motion to a position opposite the opponent's rear knee. The palm of the hand is supinated or facing upward.

Offensive Actions

Riposte. The *riposte* is a return or offensive attack following a successful parry. By executing a riposte, the defender has an opportunity to touch his opponent who might be in a poor defensive position after his offensive attempt failed. The most common riposte is a direct or immediate riposte which entails a rapid thrust following the rebound from a parry.

Simple Attacks

Simple attacks involve only one continuous action either in the line of engagement or to a line opposite the original line of engagement. The most commonly used are the straight thrust, the disengagement and the cut-over.

Straight Thrust. This movement involves a direct extension of the foil arm in the opponent's unprotected line. The arm must be extended fully without hesitation in order to eliminate loss of touch due to insufficient reach. A lunge may be necessary depending upon the distance of the opponent.

Disengagement. A disengagement is employed when the line in which you are engaged is closed or guarded. This is accomplished by passing the point and guiding it under the opponent's blade in a small circular motion into the open line. As the tip of the foil passes under the opponent's blade, the foil arm is simultaneously extended as the attacker lunges into the open line.

Cut-over. The cut-over or "coupe" is employed when your opponent maintains a low guard position. The movement is performed by lifting the point in an inverted "V" movement until it passes over the opponent's blade; the blade then moves to an open line immediately upon passing close to the opponent's blade by a full extension on the downward movement followed by a lunge.

Compound Attacks

Compound attacks involve two or more blade movements. The first movement is a preparatory action or prelude to the actual attack; it serves to draw the opponent into making a defensive move, thus opening up a line for the final or thrusting part of the attack. The most commonly used preparatory actions are the feint and the beat.

Feint. The *feint* is merely a fake attack that simulates the actual maneuver in order to draw a defensive response. As the opponent attempts to parry the false attack, the line to which the real attack will be made will open and expose itself to a touch.

Beat. The *beat* is a sharp spanking action to the foible of your opponent's blade. The action may be very strong in order to push away the opponent's blade and thus open a line, or it may be weak eliciting a parrying action from your opponent, which can be followed by a disengagement into the opposite line.

The Remise. The *remise* is a continuation of attack or a second attempt to hit an opponent after the initial attack failed and the opponent neglected to riposte. The remise is performed by replacing the point on the target without changing lines and without withdrawing the foil arm.

Right of Way. This is a rule rather than a skill that deals with the regulation of sequence during a fencing match. If the tip of the weapons were not blunted, as in earlier times, the fencer being attacked would immediately try to avoid being hit before attempting an offensive maneuver of his own. This is the basis for the rule being termed *right of way.* The fencer who first extends his foil arm with his point threatening the target is considered an attacker and has the right of way; in this situation, his opponent is then obligated to defend himself by parrying or retreating before he can assume the right of way and take up the attack. If the defender executes a successful parry, he then can assume the right of way and become the attacker by initiating a riposte. If the riposte is delayed, the original attacker is entitled to resume the offensive. In this way, the attack passes back-and-forth from one fencer to the other. Several of these exchanges of movements, called "phrases," may occur before a hit is finally scored.

RULES

Scoring and Target

To win a bout, a fencer must score five valid touches upon his opponent's target. Four touches are required in women's fencing matches. The targets for men and women are the same. In foil fencing the target excludes the limbs and head and is confined to the torso. Specifically, the valid target is the torso from the collar to a horizontal line which joins the tops of the hips across the back, and to the groin line in front. The bib of the mask is also an invalid target area. Hits which arrive off target stop all subsequent action and no hit may follow. In order for a touch to be considered legal and valid, the point of the foil must be thrust in a forward movement so that the hit would puncture the skin if the point were sharp. All slaps or hits made with the side of the blade are considered misses and action should continue.

Boundary Lines and Awarding of Touches

The piste measures forty feet long by six feet wide. A one meter extension runs from the end boundary lines in order to provide room for a fencer to retreat out of bounds without danger of tripping off the mat. When the rear foot of a retreating fencer reaches the warning line, the Director must immediately call "halt" and warn the fencer of his position. If, after this warning, the fencer retreats beyond the end boundary line with both feet, a point is scored against him. If a fencer crosses the end-line without having been warned, he will be put on guard at the warning line without penalty. If a fencer steps off the side of the piste with both feet, the Director halts the bout and replaces the fencer on the strip one yard back of the point from which he left the fencing strip.

Officiating a Bout

The conduct of a bout and all decisions concerned with the awarding of touches are the responsibility of the "jury," which is made up of four judges and one Director. The Director is in charge of the bout and has the final word regarding decisions of the jury. At his command "On-Guard," the fencers come to a guard position; upon the command "Fence," the contestants begin to fence until he calls "Halt." Once a touch has been made, a judge should immediately raise his arm to attract the attention of the Director. Upon seeing the raised hand, the Director calls a halt to the bout. After a brief reconstruction of the action which led up to the possible touch, the Director should question the judges as to the materiality of hits and resolve the question of right-of-way. Each judge has four possible ways to vote: (a) yes touch; (b) no touch; (c) off-target touch; and (d) abstain, meaning the judge was unable to see the point of the attacking blade and cannot give an opinion. Each judge's vote has a value of one point. The Director's vote, which should always be given last, has a value of one and one-half points. The abstention votes are not weighed and whether or not the point is awarded is decided by the majority of votes cast.

If a touch is awarded, the fencers are placed on guard back at the on-guard lines. If the jury decides against a valid touch, the fencers are placed on-guard where play was halted. After every hit is scored, the fencers change ends of the piste.

TERMINOLOGY

Absence of Blade—When the blades are not engaged or touching.

Advance—A forward movement toward your opponent from the guard position.

A.F.L.A.—Amateur Fencers League of America; this is the governing body of amateur fencing in America.

Attack—An attempt to contact the opponent's target with a simple or compound blade action.

Balestra—A jump-lunge attack.

Beat—A sharp tap against opponent's blade (forte to foible), to remove blade or elicit a response.

Bell-Guard—The bell shaped cup between handle and blade which protects foil hand.

Change of Engagement—The movement of the blade from one line of engagement to another.

Closed Line—A line which is protected by a guard position.

Compound Attack—Any offensive blade action consisting of two or more movements.

Corps-a-Corps—(Body to body) A closing of the guards so that fencing actions become impossible.

Coupe (Cut-over)—A simple attack which is performed by quickly passing one's foil over the opponent's foil into an open line.

Direct—An attack or parry made without changing lines.

Director—President who presides over a jury during a bout.

Disengage—A simple attack performed by passing one's blade under the opponent's blade into an open line.

Engagement—The contact when two opposing blades touch.

Feint—A false attack used to draw a response.

Foible—The weaker and more flexible portion of the blade nearest the tip.

Forte—The stronger and more rigid portion of the blade nearest the bell guard.

Grip—Portion of foil behind bell guard which a fencer handles.

Guard Position—The basic position of readiness.

Indirect—An attack, parry or riposte performed in a line other than the original line of engagement.

Judge—A member of the official jury who signals and decides upon valid touches.

Lines—The four sections of the target: high inside, high outside, low inside and low outside.

Lunge—A movement consisting of an extension from the guard position in order to reach your opponent's target.

Mask—Protective wire helmet which is worn on the head during a fencing match.

Off-Target Hit—A hit that contacts an invalid target area.

Parry—A defensive movement employed to deflect an attacking blade.

Phrase—An uninterrupted sequence of fencing action.

Piste—Fencing strip.

Pommel—Metal counter weight at the end of the handle which serves to balance the weapon as well as hold all the parts of the foil together.

Recovery—A forward or reverse movement following a lunge to the guard position.

Remise—An immediate continuation of an attack which failed, performed without withdrawing the arm.

Reprise—A new attack which follows after returning to the guard position.

Retreat—A backward movement away from one's opponent.

Right of Way—The right to assume the offensive which is gained by the fencer who first extends his foil arm with the point threatening his opponent's target or by parrying an attack.

Riposte—The counter attack used by a fencer who has executed a successful parry.

Salute—Formal gesture of courtesy used to acknowledge the opponent and the officials.

Simple Attack—An attack consisting of just one movement.

Straight Thrust—A simple direct thrust without a change in line.

Touch—A valid hit made with the blade tip against the opponent's target.

BIBLIOGRAPHY

Amateur Fencers League of America. *Fencing Rules and Manual.* Ed. Jose R. deCapriles. Worcester, Massachusetts: Hefferman Press, Inc., 1965.

Bower, Muriel, and Torao Mori. *Fencing.* Dubuque, Iowa: William C. Brown Company Publishers, 1966.

Castello, Julio Martinez. *The Theory and Practice of Fencing.* New York: Charles Scribner's Sons, 1933.

Crosnier, Roger. *Fencing with the Foil.* New York: The Ronald Press Co., 1951.

Curry, Nancy L. *Fencing.* California: Goodyear Publishing Company, Inc., 1969.

Simonian, Charles. *Fencing Fundamentals.* Columbus, Ohio: Charles E. Merrill Publishing Company, 1968.

GOLF

BEHAVIORAL OBJECTIVES

1. Given a set of golf clubs, under simulated course conditions, the college student will be able to successfully demonstrate (meet *all* of the essential criteria as specified in the chapter) the following golfing fundamentals:
   a. Nonjoining Grip.
   b. Interlocking Grip.
   c. Overlapping Grip.
   d. Square Stance.
   e. Open Stance.
   f. Closed Stance.
   g. Address.
   h. Drive Swing.
   i. Iron Shot Swing.
   j. Pitch Shot Swing.
   k. Chip Shot Swing.
   l. Sand Shot Swing.
   m. Putting Stroke.
2. The college student will be able to achieve a score of at least 75 per cent on a written examination concerned with the history, rules, terminology and analysis of golfing fundamentals.

HISTORY OF GOLF

Golf has no definite date of origin, however historians readily agree that golf started in Holland or in the low countries. During the 15th century, Scotland and England laid the groundwork for the game of golf as we know it today. The game of golf became so popular in Scotland that King James II and the Scottish Parliament banned golf in 1457. They felt that golf would jeopardize the nation's defense by diverting men away from the military sport of

archery. However, the Scot's enduring interest led to golf's refine-
ment and to the point of using various clubs to hit a ball over an
undulating course to a hole in the ground. England and Scotland are
the two countries which did most to develop the sport of golf.

The first golf courses in the United States were built around the
year 1810. For the next one hundred years golf grew slowly in the
United States and was generally looked upon as a rich man's sport.
After World War I, golf began to grow at a tremendous rate. Today
golf is one of the most popular participation sports among the
middle aged man and woman in this country.

NATURE OF GOLF

Golf is played on a grass surface which is referred to as the golf
course. The course usually consists of eighteen holes, with the distance usually ranging from one hundred to over five hundred yards
per hole. The objective of golf is to hit the golf ball from the tee into
a hole on the green in as few strokes as possible. Each hole starts at a
teeing ground which is an area specified by two markers. Play starts
by hitting the ball from a small peg, called a *tee*, which is used to
elevate the ball. A well-kept portion of grass terrain between the tee
and the green is referred to as the *fairway*. Flanking the fairway is a
heavy long grass, usually ranging from two to six inches in height,
called the *rough*. As may be expected, it is usually more difficult to
hit a ball from the rough than from the fairway. The hole is located
on a short meticulously maintained grass surface called the *green.*
The hole is actually a round cup placed in the ground which is four
and one-half inches in diameter. There are numerous hazards which
can be encountered before arriving at the green. (See Figure 6-1) The
objective of the game is to hit the golf ball from the tee to the cup
on the green in as few strokes as possible.

Competition can be provided by playing an opponent in various
ways. The type of play in which the winner is determined by the
number of holes won is called *match play*. In match play, the match
is ended when a player has won more holes from his opponent than
there are holes remaining to play. For example, when a player has
won four more holes than his opponent and there are only three
holes remaining to be played, the match ends with the score four and
three. Likewise, the match would end if a golfer was ahead of his
opponent by five holes with four holes to play. *Stroke play* is a
match where the winner is decided on the total amount of strokes
taken on a specific amount of holes (usually eighteen). Another type

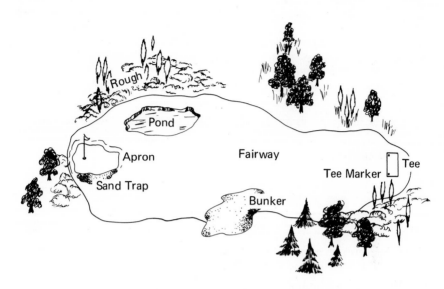

Figure 6-1. Typical Golf Course Design.

of play in which three points are awarded, one for the lowest score for each nine and one for the entire eighteen holes, whether by stroke or much play, is called *Nassau play.*

The score is computed by the number of strokes required to hit the ball from the tee to the cup. *Par* is the term used mostly in scoring. Par is computed on the distances an expert is capable of hitting a ball, and allows for two putts on each green. The distances listed in Table 6-1 are usually the bases for determining par for a hole.

The distances are not always definite in the determination of par, because consideration must be given to the relative difficulty of each hole. For example, a hole 460 yards long may be a par five because of the number and placement of hazards. Scores that are under or

TABLE 6–1

Men			Women		
Yards		Par	Yards		Par
Up to 250 yards	—	3 strokes	Up to 210 yards	—	3 strokes
251 to 470 yards	—	4 strokes	211 to 400 yards	—	4 strokes
471—up	—	5 strokes	401 to 575 yards	—	5 strokes
			576—up	—	6 strokes

over par figures are described in the following manner: *double eagle*—three strokes under par; *eagle*—two under par; *birdie*—one under par; *bogie*—one stroke over par; *double bogey*—two over par and *triple bogey*—three over par.

EQUIPMENT

The basic equipment necessary to play the game of golf consists of a set of clubs, golf balls, a golf bag, tees, and the proper clothing. Convenience gear such as motor carts, pull carts, and ball retrievers are used but not necessary.

Clubs

The two basic types of golf clubs are *woods* and *irons.* A full set of clubs consists of fourteen. However, there is no need for the beginning golfer to have a full set. A novice can learn to play the game quite well with a putter, five irons (numbers 3, 5, 7, 9, wedge), and two woods (numbers 1, 3).

The irons are generally shorter than the woods with various degrees of slant for each club face. The higher the number of the club (numbers are on the soles of the clubs), the greater the loft of the club face. The *driver* (#1 wood) has a larger head than the other woods with a face which is practically vertical. The relatively straight face and the long shaft of the driver give the ball distance without much height. As the numbers on the woods increase, the loft of the ball increases at the expense of loosing distance but gaining accuracy. Each additional wood has a shorter shaft and a greater angle on the face, thus sacrificing distance for accuracy. The irons are numbered in the same manner as the wood, that is the higher the number the greater the angle. Therefore, the lower number irons (#2 #3) are frequently used for long shots, the medium iron (#4, #5, #6) for middle distance shots, and the short irons (#7, #8, #9) for shots closer to the green. (See Figure 6-2) Table 6-2 shows the approximate distance in yards a man or woman can hit a ball with each club.

When purchasing a set of clubs the novice golfer should base his decision on the weight and length of the club along with the price. It is wise to consult a professional who is probably best qualified to assist one in selecting his clubs. (Professionals can be contacted at most established golf courses.) Since golf clubs could last a lifetime, proper maintenance is essential. A few helpful hints are: (a) always dry the entire set of golf clubs after playing in the rain or on a wet surface; (b) do not hit a ball off a rocky or hard surface; (c) wax the heads of wooden clubs; and (d) treat and store in a dry place at the end of the season.

Figure 6-2. Golf Clubs.

TABLE 6—2

Number of Club	Women	Men
1 Wood	160—200	200—250
2 Wood	160—180	200—220
3 Wood	145—165	190—210
4 Wood	140—160	180—200
1 Iron	150—180	180—200
2 Iron	140—170	170—190
3 Iron	130—160	160—180
4 Iron	120—150	150—170
5 Iron	110—140	140—160
6 Iron	100—130	130—150
7 Iron	80—120	120—140
8 Iron	70—100	110—130
9 Iron	60— 90	100—120
Pitching Wedge	50— 80	90—110
Sand Wedge	20— 40	20— 50

Balls

Due to the over abundance of different makes and brands of golf balls, it is very difficult for the novice to make a choice when purchasing golf balls. The price will range from 35 cents to $1.25 each. The novice should purchase balls in the cheaper price range since he is more likely to lose or deface the cover of his ball. The cheaper priced ball will generally have a thicker cover and a lower compression, thus cutting down on the distance. However, the distance lost is no great hardship. In order for balls to maintain their true flight and to be easily visible, they should be kept clean at all times.

Practice golf balls made of various materials, such as plastic, rubber, and cotton can be helpful when practicing. Several advantages of practicing with these balls are that they are economical, durable, and travel a short distance, thus allowing one to practice hitting considerably more balls.

Golf Bags

A golf bag is needed to carry the golf clubs, balls, and possibly other items such as wearing apparel. It is usually best to purchase a light-weight bag with compartments for each club. The reasons are that there will be less wear and tear on the club heads if they are in separate compartments. Also, it is much easier to carry a light bag around a course for approximately five or six miles.

Tees and Clothing

Tees are made from many different materials—plastic and wood are the most popular and inexpensive. A person who expects to play golf more than a few times a year should purchase some essential wearing apparel. In order to prevent blisters and calluses or for the sake of general comfort, proper shoes should be worn. Also, a good pair of shoes with spikes is essential to prevent slipping when address-ing and hitting the ball. A right-handed golfer should wear a golf glove on his left hand for the same purposes as stated for the shoes. It is also important to wear loose-fitting shirts and trousers. Jewelry such as rings should not be worn because of the grip being hindered. Bracelets and watches are not only hazardous and sometimes danger-ous, but they are also subject to damage.

SKILLS TO BE DEVELOPED

The golf swing is not a basic familiar fundamental movement. It is an unnatural movement which must be learned. The basic move-ments are the same for swinging all the clubs except for the putting motion. Also, the golf swing cannot be learned in parts or taken apart and learned in progression. It must be a cohesive movement in which each phase is dependent on the other phases for proper execu-tion. Although the grip, stance, backswing, downswing, and follow-through can be discussed in parts, they must be completely coordi-nated into one complete movement.

There are many skills which one must learn about the game of golf. These skills include learning how to judge distances, how to relax, knowing which club to use, ability to read the contour of greens, among various other skills. However, the single most im-portant factor is perfecting the golf swing. Although there is no one correct style for every individual, there are some pertinent basic fundamentals involved in each part of the swing.

The Grip

A correct grip is a fundamental necessity in the golf swing. The club must be held correctly before it becomes physically possible to swing it correctly.

In the correct grip, the two hands should function as nearly as possible as one, and their placement should encourage easy handling of the club throughout the swing. The student must also maintain a fixed relation throughout the swing between his hands and the face of the club. The shaft may not turn in his hands while he is making the stroke. The grip must be positive and firm but not strained.

In order to acquire the proper grip for the right-handed golfer, allow the sole of the clubhead to rest on the ground. Allow the grip of the club to rest diagonally across the middle of the left hand, from the second joint of the forefinger to the heel of the hand. Next, wrap the fingers around the grip with the thumb pointing down and slightly to the right side of the shaft. Approximately one-half of an inch of the shaft should extend beyond the left hand in order to give better balance and freedom of movement.

The next step is to place the right hand below the left, with the fold in front of the heel of the right hand covering the left thumb. Wrap the forefinger of the right hand around the club in the same manner as a trigger finger. The grip should now be resting across the first joint of the forefinger and the hand, at a junction of the other fingers and the palm on the right hand. Next, close the hand in much the same manner as shaking hands. The right thumb should be slightly to the left of the center of the grip meeting the right forefinger. Be sure the hand grip is firm but not strained.

There are three different methods for joining the little finger of the right hand with the forefinger of the left.

Baseball (Nonjoining) Grip. Both hands grip the club in a manner in which the eight fingers are in contact with the grip. Although the fingers do not overlap, they should be as close together as possible. This grip is the least desirable, but may be used by students with weak wrists or short fingers. (See Figure 6-3a)

Interlocking Grip. In the interlocking grip, the forefinger of the left hand interlocks with the little finger of the right hand. Thus, six fingers contact the grip. (See Figure 6-3b)

Overlapping Grip. In this grip, the little finger of the right hand overlaps and grips the left forefinger. (See Figure 6-3c) The interlock-

a. baseball   b. interlocking   c. overlapping

Figure 6-3. The Grip.

ing and overlapping grips are both considered sound, however most experts appear to prefer the overlapping grip.

In each of the three grips, the club should be held by the fingers and not in the palm. Since no two students have hands exactly the same, it is impossible to say one grip is best for everyone. The student should experiment until he finds the grip that feels most comfortable.

Address and Stance

Beginning to play a golf shot is addressing the ball and the posture one assumes is the stance. Essentials of the stance position are ease, comfort, and relaxation.

In order to be consistent in hitting the ball, there are several principles which should be followed. These principles are concerned with a stable body being perfectly balanced over the feet. Balance of the body must be maintained even when shifting the weight from one foot to another.

The following three types of stances are used when hitting a golf ball: (a) the square; (b) the open; (c) the closed. These terms describe the foot placement in relation to the prescribed line of flight of the ball. In all instances, the toes are pointed slightly outward. In the square stance, the feet are directly parallel to the intended line of flight of the ball. The closed stance finds the left foot closer to the direction of flight line than the right foot. In the open stance, the right foot is closer to the line of direction than the left foot and the body is turned slightly toward the hole. (See Figure 6-4) The foot position chosen depends upon the type of swing needed, the club to be used, and the intended flight of the ball.

The type of stance used is related to the type of club. The open stance is usually used when hitting short iron shots. This stance allows for less rotation of the body and a shorter backswing and thus a better controlled shot. The square stance is employed for the middle distance iron shots. This stance permits more hip rotation than the open stance and thus more power but less accuracy. When driving from the tee or hitting long fairway shots the closed stance is employed. This stance allows for even more power with the risk of sacrificing some accuracy.

When addressing the ball, the sole of the clubs should be placed on the ground directly behind the ball. Regardless of the grip or stance employed, the left arm is extended with the right elbow bent slightly. Both elbows should point toward the belt line while bending slightly at the waist. The golfer must now try to relax with a confident comfortable feeling.

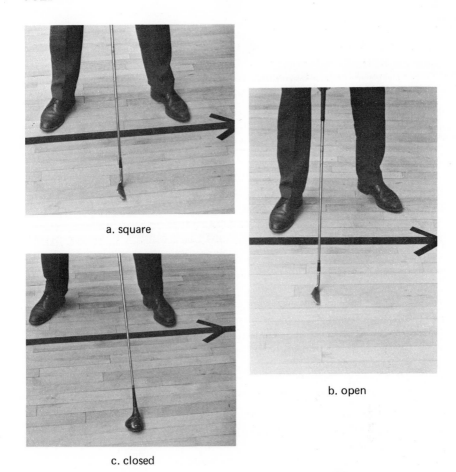

a. square

b. open

c. closed

Figure 6-4. The Stance.

In order to have a smooth coordinated swing, it is important to have a firm base. The feet should be spread comfortably apart with the weight shifted slightly inward and to the balls of the feet. Next, flex the knees slightly while focusing the eyes on the ball. The head must stay fixed over the ball throughout the entire swing. The shoulders and hips rotate, however the head must stay completely stationary. We are now ready to hit the little white "critter." (See Figure 6-5)

Backswing

The purpose of the backswing is to establish a perfectly balanced position at the top of the swing from which the correct actions of the downstroke can flow rhythmically and without the need for correction. Actually, the downswing of the club should be in the same arc as the backswing.

In order to bring the club back properly, slowly pull the club with the shoulders and arms along a straight line from the ball until the hands are in front of the right leg. Slowly shift the weight to the right leg, allowing the left knee to move in and slightly down in a direction behind the ball. The right leg should remain straight in a balanced position. The body should rotate around the head and feet.

At a point just before the hands reach the right leg, the student should lift the clubhead by cocking the wrists. The clubhead should continue in an upward arc until the left shoulder is under the eyes which are focused on the ball. Throughout the entire backswing, the right elbow should be pointing toward the ground. At the top of the backswing, the weight should shift mostly to the back leg. Now, the student is ready for the downswing. (See Figure 6-6)

Downswing and Follow-Through

As contact is made with the ball, the wrists must be firm in order to allow the full impact of the body's uncoiling action to be trans-

Figure 6-5. Address.   Figure 6-6. Backswing.

mitted through the clubhead to the ball. The left knee is relaxed as the weight is transferred back to the left leg. A stable head and base must be maintained as the shoulders and hips rotate. The emphasis for irons is almost always on a strong downward swing. The face of the club descends down hitting the ball and continuing down into the turf.

The momentum of the swing carries the clubhead through the rest of the arc over the left shoulder. The key to a successful swing is to let the clubhead follow in the direction of the ball as long as possible. (See Figure 6-7) At the end of the swing the body weight should be mostly on the ball of the left foot and not on the heel. (See Figure 6-8)

Figure 6-7. Follow-through.   Figure 6-8. Completed
                                               Follow-through.

In many instances a player will have to hit a ball while standing on uneven terrain. As a general rule when playing an uphill or down hill lie, play the ball off or near the uphill foot. For an uphill lie use a club one number lower than usual because the ball will be hit higher than normal and thus some loss of distance. The reverse is true of a down hill lie.

When the ball is higher than the feet, choke up on the grip slightly to equalize the height of the ball with the feet. The player should also allow for a hook rather than try to change the swing in order to hit a straight ball. Provided the ball is lower than the feet, stand closer to the ball and allow for a slight slice.

Pitching

A pitch shot is employed when the ball is a few feet to approximately eighty yards from the green. A high number iron or a wedge is used to give the ball height and backspin. The shot should be high and land near the pin; the backspin should keep the ball near the pin.

The golfer should use an open stance with the feet approximately one foot apart and the knees flexed. The ball should be played off a line parallel with the inside of the right heel. The wrists and arms do most of the work with little body movement. The club must be lifted rather sharply in order to hit sharply down and through the ball. As in all shots, the clubhead should follow a line toward the flag. Do not try to scoop or lift the ball with the clubhead.

Important points to remember when pitching are: to use an open stance with the feet about one foot apart, to lift the club sharply on the backswing, to make the downswing and follow-through short and crisp, to contact the ball before the turf, and to hit down and through the ball.

Chipping

A chip shot is used when the ball is resting a few feet from the green and the terrain is too uneven to use a putter. The chip shot is usually made with a middle number iron. The club number is determined by variables such as the length of grass, hitting up or down hill, and the general slope of the green.

The golfer should use an open stance with the knees bent slightly. The wrists stay quite firm with little body movement. The stroke is performed mostly with the wrists and arms. The ball is hit with a sweeping motion (not chopping) with the clubhead staying close to the ground and following the line of the ball.

Important points to remember when chipping are: to use an open stance, play the ball off the heel of the right foot, have a firm left wrist at contact, follow through the path of the ball, use mostly wrist and arm movement, and sweep through the ball.

Sand Traps

Even though the sand trap shot is one of the most feared golf shots, it can be one of the easiest. It is important in the sand shot, as in all shots, to have a firm base. Thus the golfer should dig in with both feet while using an open stance.

At no time may the clubhead touch the sand before the swing. The objective is to hit the sand slightly behind the ball and not the ball directly. The shot is done mostly with the wrists and arms. The swing is usually an outside to inside swing with the wrists cocked sharply. The clubhead must cut the sand behind the ball and follow through with the clubhead following the intended line of the ball. Do not punch the shot or try to hit the ball without hitting the sand. A full follow-through is required.

Important points to remember when hitting from sand traps are: to use an open stance, plant the feet into the sand to secure a firm base, swing from the outside to the inside, cock the wrists on the backswing, have firm wrists upon contact, slice the club into the sand slightly behind the ball, and always follow through.

Putting

Putting is a very important part of golf. In order to have a good score, the golfer must putt well. There is no one best way to grip a club or way to stand while putting. However, there are some basic principles which should be followed. Generally, the head is placed directly over the ball with a locked stance which prevents body movement. The club grip is held primarily by the fingers. The stroke is straight back and then forward hitting through the ball with the clubhead going in a straight line with the initial intended line of the ball. Short putts should be just tapped with a short backswing and little follow through.

There is no best stance. However, most authorities recommend a slightly open stance with the ball played off the left heel and the weight slightly shifted to the left foot. The regular overlapping grip is used quite extensively. However, the most popular grip is the reverse overlap. For the reverse overlapping grip, the first finger of the left hand overlaps the little finger of the right hand.

The mental portion of putting is as important as the physical. The golfer must be able to read the contour of the green, be able to relax, concentrate, and putt with confidence.

Important points to remember when putting are: use any stance that is comfortable but limits body movement, use only a wrist and arm movement, hold your head directly over the ball, hold the club lightly but firmly, bring the clubhead back slowly and close to the grass, follow through with a smooth forward stroke (except on short putts), and keep the hands even with the ball at contact.

RULES

The official rules of golf in the United States for men and women are established by the United States Golf Association. The established rules are designed to protect golfers in addition to provide uniformity to the game.

Etiquette

Golf is generally a social game. The sport of golf has developed a universal code of fair play and sportsmanship. Some of the most important principles which provide us with golf etiquette are:

1. Be considerate to all golfers, regardless of playing ability.
2. Do not yell at any time on the course except for the warning yell of "Fore."
3. Whenever possible play without delay.
4. Do not talk while a golfer is hitting.
5. Replace all divots.
6. Do not hit while players are in range.
7. When searching for a lost ball, allow other players to pass. Do not continue until they are out of range.
8. Do not search for a ball longer than five minutes if golfers are behind you.
9. Rake all foot-marks made in a sand trap.
10. Inform your opponents if you deserve a penalty.
11. Allow the player who earned the honor to hit first.
12. Do not step or cast a shadow on a golfer's putting line.
13. While at the teeing ground, do not talk and stand away from the person driving.
14. Do not place bags, carts, or other materials on the green. Try to prevent damage to the green by fixing all ball marks and always gently laying the flagstick down.

General Rules

1. The golfer is allowed to have fourteen or less clubs in his bag.
2. The ball must always be teed up within the tee markers when starting a hole. The golfer must also stand in an area between and in back of the markers; however, no more than two club lengths behind the markers.
3. A ball knocked off a tee accidentally is re-teed with no penalty.

4. A ball is considered as lost or out of bounds after searching for five minutes. The penalty is loss of distance plus one stroke.
5. The lie of a ball may not be improved, unless playing winter rules. Various objects touching or near the ball such as leaves, twigs, and pop bottles may be moved.
6. A golfer may not touch his club to the sand at any time before hitting the ball while in a hazard.
7. A ball which is lying anywhere other than in a bunker may be lifted, cleaned, and replaced. The spot where the ball was lying should be marked with a commercial ball marker or a dime.
8. If a ball is in bounds, but is lying at an unplayable spot where the ground is under repair the ball should be dropped at the first reasonable spot away from the hole.

Some of the basic rules which are pertinent for the beginning golfer have been listed. There are many more intricate rules involved with the game of golf. An official rules book can be purchased from most sporting goods stores for approximately 35 cents.

TERMINOLOGY

Ace—A hole made in one stroke.
Addressing the Ball—Stance taken before hitting the ball.
Approach Shot—A shot hit with the intention of landing on the green.
Apron—Closely cut grass surrounding the green.
Away—Ball lying farthest away from the hole.
Birdie—A score of one under par for the hole.
Bite—Backspin on the ball causing it not to roll very far.
Bogey—A score of one over par for the hole.
Bunker—Depressed area usually covered with sand.
Caddie—A person who carries the clubs and assists a player as provided in the rules.
Casual Water—A temporary accumulation of water which is not recognized as a water hazard.
Cup—The hole on the putting green.
Divot—A piece of turf displaced by the clubhead during a stroke.
Dog Leg—A bend in the fairway to the right or left.
Dormie—A score in match play when a player or team is ahead of the opponent by as many holes as there are remaining to be played.
Double Bogey—A score of two strokes over par for the hole.
Double Eagle—A score of three strokes under par for the hole.
Drive—The stroke from a tee played for maximum distance.

Eagle—A score of two strokes under par for the hole.

Fade—A shot that drifts from left to right.

Fairway—The well kept grass between the tee and green.

Fore—A warning called to anyone in danger of being hit by a ball.

Foursome—Four golfers playing together.

Frog Hair—The higher grass at the apron.

Green—Well kept grass surrounding the cup (putting area).

Halved—To tie a hole or game in match play.

Handicap—The approximate number of strokes the golfer shoots over par; allowance given to equalize players of different abilities.

Hazard—A bunker, tree, or water.

Hole Out—The last stroke for a player at a hole.

Honor—The privilege of hitting first from the tee earned by achieving the lowest score on the previous hole.

Hook—A ball which curves to the left when in flight.

Lie—The position of the ball on the ground.

Match Play—A type of scoring based on the total strokes per round.

Par—An arbitrary method of scoring excellence usually based on the length of the hole plus allowing for two putts.

P.G.A.—Professional Golf Association (for men).

Playing Through—The courtesy of letting a faster group pass ahead of a slower group.

Press—Attempting to hit the ball too hard.

Provisional Ball—A second ball played because the first ball hit may be out of bounds or lost.

Pull—A shot hit on a straight line to the left of the green.

Push—A shot hit on a straight line to the right of the green.

Rough—The fairly long grass on either side of the fairway.

Scratch Player—A player who has a handicap of zero.

Slice—A ball which curves to the right.

Stance—The position of the feet while hitting the ball.

Stymie—To have another player's ball or some other object in one's intended line of play.

Tee—A peg on which the ball is placed when starting a new hole.

Teeing Ground—The designated starting place for a hole.

U.S.G.A.—United States Golf Association.

Winter Rules—Special local rules to improve the lie of the ball on the fairway. This is a seasonal rule when the fairways are not in the best of shape.

BIBLIOGRAPHY

Ainsworth, Dorothy and others. *Individual Sports for Women.* Philadelphia: W.B. Saunders Co., 1963.

Browning, Robert. *A History of Golf.* New York: E.P. Dutton and Co., Inc., 1955.

Casper, William. *Chipping and Putting.* New York: The Ronald Press Company, 1961.

Cheatum, Billye Ann. *Golf.* Philadelphia: W.B. Saunders Co., 1969.

Nance, Virginia L. and E.C. Davis. *Golf.* Dubuque, Iowa: William C. Brown Company Publishers, 1966.

Platte, Jules, and Herb Graffis. *Better Golf Through Better Practice.* Englewood Cliffs, New Jersey: Prentice Hall, Inc., 1958.

Player, Gary. *Positive Golf: Understanding and Applying the Fundamentals of the Game.* New York: McGraw-Hill Book Company, 1967.

United States Golf Association. *The Official Rules of Golf.* 40 E. 38th St., New York: 1971.

CHAPTER

7

HORSEMANSHIP

BEHAVIORAL OBJECTIVES

1. Given a horse, the college student will be able to successfully demonstrate (meet *all* of the essential criteria as specified in the chapter) the following horsemanship fundamentals:
   a. Tack an English Saddle.
   b. Untack an English Saddle.
   c. Mounting.
   d. Dismounting.
   e. Hands.
   f. Seat.
   g. Balance.
2. Given a horse, the college student will be able to ride at a walk for a distance of 100 yards.
3. From a walk, the college student will be able to stop and back four paces.
4. Given a horse, the college student will be able to ride at a trot for a distance of 100 yards.
5. From a trot, the college student will be able to stop to a standstill.
6. Given a horse, the college student will be able to ride at a canter for a distance of 300 yards.
7. From a canter, the college student will be able to change gaits to a trot, and then to a walk and finally come to a complete stop.
8. Given a horse, the college student will be able to ride in one figure-8 at a walk to the right and then to the left.
9. Given a horse, the college student will be able to ride in two figure-8's at a trot to the right, posting with proper balance.
10. Given a horse, the college student will be able to ride in three figure-8's at a canter to the right and then to the left on proper lead.
11. The college student will be able to achieve a score of at least 75

per cent on a written examination concerned with the proper care and selection of horsemanship tack, psychology of horsemanship, safety and analysis of horsemanship fundamentals.

INTRODUCTION

The chapter is written basically for the person who has done little or no riding. When read, its purpose is to assist a person who would like to begin his experiences as a rider, and needs enough help to give him a start. It is not intended to clutter one's mind with all the facts that it has taken an experienced rider years to learn.

Every horseman has his own approach to riding, and some of his own ways of doing things. This chapter will concentrate on the most generally accepted practices.

Very generally, beginning riders fall into these two categories: those who are afraid, shy, and timid; and those who feel there is nothing to it. Either way, people in these two categories run the risk of being injured or frightened, which could possibly cause them to end their riding career. This chapter will take the common sense approach to horsemanship and will endeavor to eliminate the categories mentioned above.

"Safety first" is a slogan used in conjunction with many sports of a recreational nature. Boating, camping and skiing enthusiasts all are bombarded with material on the safety aspects of their respective sport. They all have their potential dangers when people are careless or use faulty equipment. In riding, we have one added variable which does not exist in most of the other recreational sports. We are on an animal with a mind of his own. He has greater body size and more strength than we as a rider have. We cannot muscle the animal into doing things and therefore must use another approach.

There are several ways in which a person can obtain access to a horse and learn to ride. He could be lucky enough to have a friend who has a horse and is willing to teach him. He could have, in his college curriculum, a course in horsemanship. Or, he could go to a local stable for a mount and instruction.

Learning to ride is no more costly than learning to play golf. But, there are some concerns you should have in mind when selecting a course or stable in which to take instruction.

First of all, check to see if the facility is clean and neatly kept. The stalls should be clean, aisleways clear and equipment put away. The horses should be well groomed and should not have long hair caked with mud. The tack (saddles and bridles), should be clean and soft as opposed to dirty, dry and brittle.

Some of the things mentioned above will be discussed in some detail later. It is felt that if a riding facility has the clean qualities mentioned above, that the management cares for its horses and that they probably provide good instruction.

NATURE OF HORSEMANSHIP

Horses come in many different personality types, just as people do. Some are easy going, have good dispositions and are good to use as school horses. Others may have one or more little idiosyncrasies. For example, a horse may be difficult to bridle, but in every other aspect be fine. On the other hand, some horses should only be handled by experienced riders.

Horses that are used by riding schools and other instructive facilities are usually well schooled and the instructors are versed in suiting their horses to the riders. In being suited, it is meant that the personality of the horse and rider are compatible and that they can cooperate with each other in full confidence.

Cooperation and confidence in learning to ride are two important aspects. If a novice rider is put on, or tries a horse that is too much for him, he is bound to wind up in trouble. The horse will sense his lack of confidence. On the other hand, a bold rider could be put on a horse who is not ready, or not schooled enough, to do the things that the rider is. In this case, a rider could force a horse to jump who is not ready and could retard the development and schooling of the horse. The rider should use good judgement at all times so the horse will develop a trust in him.

Horses are bred to obtain different sizes and qualities to perform varied functions. Some of these functions include racing, fox hunting, polo, showing, work or draft and pleasure riding. In the west horses are used on the ranges to move and to cut cattle. These western horses are called *quarter horses* and are average sized so they may turn, stop, and cut on a dime. The name quarter horse comes from the fact that these horses are exceptionally fast at a quarter mile.

The *thoroughbred* is a pure strain, bred for speed, and larger size than the quarter horse. They are a fine wiry breed and are raced on the flat track or steeplechase. They have stamina and also make excellent hunters. Thoroughbreds tend to be highly spirited especially when highly conditioned. One usually does not find a thoroughbred in a riding stable where people go and rent horses out.

For one thing they are expensive and the price goes up with the royalty of their blood lines. For instance, a colt by Man-of-War out of a good mare would be extremely expensive.

A common bred horse is one where there is a mixture in the breeding. These horses are cheaper and will be found in riding stables. They don't make good race horses because they don't have the fineness and speed bred into them. They are usually quieter and are excellent pleasure horses. Some make good hunters. A *half bred horse*, which is becoming popular in the hunt field, is a mixture of thoroughbred and quarter horse. It has good size, has the speed and stamina of the thoroughbred and the quick toughness of the quarter horse.

The *standard bred horse* was one developed in this country and primarily used for trotting and pacing races. They are exceptionally fast at these gaits. This type of racing started back when these horses were used to pull light carts and proud men would match their horse against others.

The American Saddle horse is one of the most beautiful breeds. This horse has a combination of the good points of all the other breeds. They are versatile and can be used to pleasure ride, drive or show. In the show ring they are fiery, and have extremely animated gaits. They have a majestic carriage and are aesthetically pleasing to watch.

The breeds mentioned above are just a few of the many types and breeds of horses. These were selected for discussion because they are the most common. There are many books available on the types, breeds and uses of horses if one is interested in further information.

It is good, at the start, to learn the parts and points of reference of the horse's anatomy. Then when you are discussing horses you will know the points being talked about and can converse intelligently. The diagram labels the horse with the most useful parts. (See Figure 7-1)

A horse's height is measured in *hands.* A hand is equivalent to four inches. This measurement is taken from the ground to the top of the withers and is done with a special measuring stick with the hands indicated on it.

Any horse under fourteen hands two inches is considered a pony. An average size horse is from fifteen to sixteen hands. A horse this size can weigh between nine hundred to fourteen hundred pounds.

At birth, a horse is called a *foal.* A foal can be either a *colt* (male) or a *filly* (female). When the foal is weaned from its dam, or mother, it is called a weanling. This takes place at about six months. After its first year it is called a *yearling* and then a two-year-old. A filly is

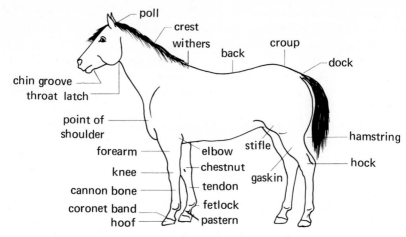

Figure 7-1. Anatomy Chart.

called a *mare* after four years of age. A stallion who has been castrated is called a *gelding*. A gelding is usually more passive and easier to handle than a stallion. A horse is left a stallion and used as a stud if he has good breeding and has done well performance-wise himself.

Care and Grooming of the Horse

Grooming is an essential part of the care of a horse. A horse that is in use should be groomed every day and especially before being ridden. This care improves the appearance of the horse, protects him against parasites and skin disease, and helps the condition of his skin and hair.

A horse should never be ridden before being cleaned. The dirt under the back can cause irritation and sore spots may occur. Cleaning the horse is half the fun of working with him and getting to know him. It is part of horsemanship. There is not much sense in knowing how to ride without knowing how to care for the animal you are riding.

Here is a very simple process to follow when grooming a horse: (a) Begin with currying which is done with a curry comb made of hard rubber. Curry in circles very briskly. This is done to raise the dirt and loosen any caked mud. Go all over the horse's body except for the head where a softer brush will be used. Be gentle around the flank and stifle. This is a sensitive area and the horse may kick. (b) Next, you brush the horse with a dandy brush which has stiff bristles. The brushing is done in the direction that the hair grows and with short hard strokes. Brush all the way down the leg to the hoof.

Make sure you brush both sides of the leg. The inside is often neglected. (c) Then, we have two finishing touches which you should use when being very particular. One is using the body brush after the dandy brush. This is a softer, shorter bristled brush and serves to smooth the hair. The second is to use a rub rag or towel which removes the dust and puts a shine on the horse's coat. (See Figure 7-2)

The mane and tail should be combed with a metal toothed comb and then brushed with the dandy brush. The mane and tail should be free of knots, straw and briers. If the mane is sticking up and not well trained to one side, a water brush can be used to help keep it down and to train it. There is a small mane comb called a pulling comb which is used for braiding and pulling the mane. A mane should never be cut, it should be pulled. (See Figure 7-2)

Needless to say the horse's feet are very important and require care. His feet should be trimmed by a blacksmith every six months and his shoes reset. As part of the grooming process, you should clean any material out of his foot with a hoof pick. The pick should be run down the creases at the side of the frog (the sensitive area of the foot). The hoofs should be picked at the end of the ride to make sure the horse has not gotten any gravel, sticks or any other material that may be injurious, caught in the frog or shoe. (See Figure 7-2)

mane comb

dandy brush

hoof pick

water brush

rubber curry comb

finishing brush

pulling comb

frog

Figure 7-2. Grooming Aids.

EQUIPMENT (TACK)

Care and Safety. Tack is a term which refers to the equipment we put on the horse in order to ride. It includes the bridle, saddle and the martingale. This equipment should be properly stored and cleaned after every use. Saddles should be placed on a V-shaped rack and the bridles stored on a rounded wooden block. Manufacturers are producing open metal saddle racks which allow the bottom of the saddle to dry. (See Figure 7-3)

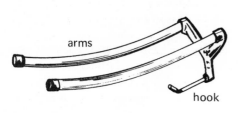

arms

hook

Figure 7-3. Saddle Rack.

Leather that is not cleaned and lubricated properly will dry out and crack. The perspiration from the horse will build up on the under side of the leather and can cause irritation to the skin. Mud and dirt can also dry the tack out.

After use, the tack should be wiped off with a damp sponge. It should be taken apart and saddle soap or Lexol applied to all the leather, making sure that the area under the buckles is covered. The metal stirrups and bits should be cleaned with metal polish.

If tack is taken care of and stored in the manner mentioned above it will last much longer and will be easier to use because it will be soft and plyable. It will also be much safer. Dried and cracked leather may break and cause an accident.

When you go to a stable to ride you should be sure to check the condition of the tack even if they tack the horse for you. Some of the most important areas to check are:

1. The girth should be checked to make sure it is snug and that the billit straps (leather straps the girth is buckled to) are in good condition.
2. Check the stirrup leathers to make sure that they are not cracked and dry looking. All your weight goes in the stirrups so the leathers must be in good shape.
3. Check the bridle and make sure all the buckles are fastened and that the reins are in good shape. Dried and cracked reins can cause blisters on the hands because they are not plyable. Check the reins where they fasten to the bit. This portion gets a lot of wear and tear from pulling and if they break you have no control of your horse.

Tacking and Untacking. Every rider should know how to tack and untack his horse. This along with grooming is all part of horsemanship. Some stables clean and tack your horse for you and therefore one never learns these aspects of working with a horse.

After the horse is cleaned you are ready to tack. We saddle and bridle the horse from his left side. This gives the horse some consistency in the tacking process. All horses who have ever been tacked are used to it. Mounting and dismounting are also done on the left side. This came about because of the side the calvary officer wore his sword. In mounting from the left it was out of the way.

There are different types of bits and bridles and this results from the fact that horses are easier to handle or go better in one type or the other.

A *snaffle bridle* is one where the bit has large rings on the sides and a jointed bar in the middle. This type of bit is one of the easiest on a horse's mouth and is used on horses who are easier to control. It has a single rein, which when pulled on, buckles the joint in the middle of the bar and applies pressure on the roof of the horse's mouth. (See Figure 7-4a)

A *pelham bridle* has a straight bar bit which can be rubber covered. This is also for a horse with a fairly easy mouth but who needs a little more control than the snaffle applies. This bit has a shaft on it and has one rein attached in rings at each side of the bit and one rein attached to rings at the end of the shaft. The lower rein is called the curb rein and when pulled on, tilts the bit forward to the roof of the mouth and the shaft back toward the body of the horse. When this happens, it applies pressure on a chain called the curb chain. The pressure is exerted on the chin groove and gives added control. (See Figure 7-4b)

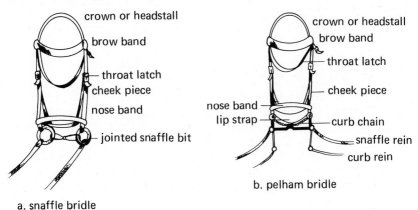

Figure 7-4. Bridles.

A *curb bit* is more severe than either the snaffle or pelham. It is a bar bit with a curve in the middle. The higher the curve, the more

severe the bit. It has shafts like the pelham and the longer the shafts the more leverage and the more severe the bit. It also has the added control of the curb chain and is used on horses that are hard or difficult to control. (See Figure 7-5)

There are many other varieties of bits depending on the severity needed. The ones mentioned above are the most common used in English riding.

To bridle, put the reins over the horse's head and remove the halter. The reins over his head gives you something to hold him with if he decides to walk away. The head stall of the halter can also be buckled around his neck to give something else to control him with. Hold the bridle by the crown or head stall with your right hand and stand beside the horse, facing his head on his left side. Hold the bit across the palm of your left hand with your finger tips facing the right side of the bridle. Pull up on the head stall and apply pressure against the teeth with the bit. Most horses will open their mouths in response to this pressure. If not, the thumb of the left hand can be inserted into his mouth behind the teeth. A downward pressure with the thumb in this area will help in opening the horse's mouth. Once the bit has been inserted in the mouth, the head stall can be placed over both ears so that it rests behind them on the poll.

Figure 7-5. Curb Bit.

At this point the bridle should be checked for adjustment. If it is too tight it will pull dimples in the corners of the horse's mouth. If it is too loose, the bit will wobble in his mouth and he will try to get it between his teeth. When properly fitted it will cross the area of the mouth just behind the teeth. If a horse can get the bit in his teeth you lose control of him and he might run away with you.

To adjust the bridle, undo the buckles on the cheek piece and raise or lower the bit as needed. If you raise it one hole on the right side you should raise it one hole on the left side. This is done to keep the bit even in the horse's mouth.

Once the bridle is in place the buckles of the throat latch and nose band can be secured. If the bridle is a pelham or double reined bridle the curb chain will also have to be hooked.

When putting the saddle on, the stirrup irons should be in their stored position. If they are not, take the stirrup and run it up the back leather until it reaches the attachment to the saddle and then put the leather through the oval opening in the stirrup. In this position, the stirrups will not be in the way when putting the saddle on. The girth should be over the top of the saddle or run through the right stirrup iron so it is not in the way. The saddle is put on from the horse's left side and is placed up on the withers so that the girth will go around just behind the front legs.

Buckle the girth loosely to the billet straps at first. As the horse is walked out of the stall or teaching area, he will adjust to the girth and will let some air out. When this happens the girth can be tightened. Also, before tightening the girth make sure the saddle pad is straight and not overlapped anywhere. This condition could rub a sore on his back. (See Figure 7-6)

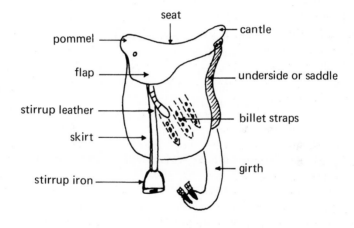

Figure 7-6. English Saddle.

Most English riders use a martingale which is a leather device that connects the noseband or reins to the girth. It is used to keep the horse's head down and to stop him from rearing. There are two basic types: the running and the standing. The running has rings which the reins go through and has more effect on the bit. The standing is attached to the noseband and works more to keep the head down. The girth is run through the loop at the end of both of these types before being fastened. (See Figure 7-7)

Tacking and untacking should be practiced until it can be done with little or no error. All buckles and straps should be checked. All

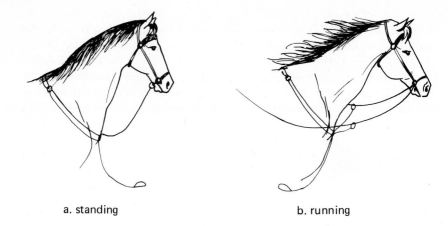

a. standing   b. running

Figure 7-7. Martingales.

the leather with its buckles and straps can be confusing to the novice. The girth should be checked before mounting. You should just be able to slide your hand under it. It should have a snug feeling. If the girth is not tight, the saddle could slide around when mounting.

SKILLS TO BE DEVELOPED

Mounting and Dismounting

There are two generally accepted ways to mount a horse: (a) facing the rear, (b) facing the head. The method of facing the head is used by saddle seat and western riders and therefore will not be discussed here. (See Figure 7-8)

To mount facing the rear, (a) stand on the left or near side of your horse about at his shoulder, (b) take up the reins in your left hand with the left rein tightened and the right rein slackened. Place the hand on top of the pommel, (c) take the stirrup iron with the right hand and turn it toward you, (d) place your left foot in the stirrup and reach around to the cantle of the saddle, (e) spring gently off the right foot and pull on the cantle and swing your right foot over the back of the horse, (f) place your right foot in the stirrup and you are on. Make sure you turn the stirrup toward the rear of the

Figure 7-8. Mounting (Facing the Rear).

horse. By turning the left and right stirrups as mentioned, the stirrup leathers lie flat along the inside of the legs and will alleviate the pinching caused by twisted leathers.

This method of mounting is considered one of the safest because the horse cannot kick you with his rear foot and he cannot bite you because your body is so close to his neck and shoulders. When mounting facing the head, if the horse walks forward, you have to stop him and try again. In mounting facing the rear, if the horse walks forward he actually helps you by moving into you.

Dismounting is almost the reverse of the mounting process: (a) take the right foot out of the stirrup, (b) place the left hand on the pommel, (c) swing the right leg over the back and place the right hand on the cantle, (d) support the weight on the arms and remove the left foot from the stirrup and drop to the ground. It must be emphasized here that the left foot is taken out of the stirrup *before* dropping to the ground. This is important because if the horse moves and throws you off balance, your foot could be caught in the stirrup, and a possibility of being dragged could result. (See Figure 7-9)

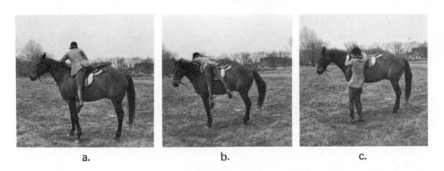

a.   b.   c.

Figure 7-9. Dismounting.

You should learn to mount without the aid of a mounting block. If you are out on the trail and have to get off, it is essential you know how to remount. If the horse is tall and you are having difficulty reaching the stirrup, put the horse on a downhill slope and you should stand on the uphill. If there is no slope, lower the stirrup so you can reach it and then return it to its original position once in the saddle.

Make sure you check the girth each time before you mount.

Holding the Reins

A beginning rider should start out with a single reined bridle or one pair of reins. If a double reined bridle is used, the curb rein can be tied off. Make sure the rein is flat from the bit to your hand and not twisted.

Wrap your fingers around the reins with the knuckles facing out and the thumb at the top. The rein behind your grip should fall over your index finger and hang down on the left side of the withers. The position of the hand is like it is when holding a tumbler of water. (See Figure 7-10)

Figure 7-10. Holding the Reins.

Now the position of the hand on the rein should be adjusted to provide for light contact with the horse's mouth. There should be a straight line from your elbow to the wrist, hand, and down the rein to the horse's mouth. The elbows should be close to the sides and the hands held just above the withers and approximately six inches apart. (See Figure 7-11)

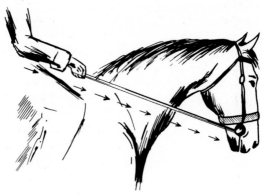

Figure 7-11. Line of Control.

Another method of holding the reins is to grip the reins in the same manner as mentioned above but turn the palm of the hand down. The difference in the reining action is that in the first method the wrists can be turned down to apply pressure on the bit and in the second the wrists can be turned outward for pressure. This wrist pressure is light control on the horse's mouth. This, plus a pulling action of the arm, will apply more force on the horse's mouth.

Beginning riders have a tendency to hold the reins too tight which results in applying constant pressure on the horse's mouth. Light hands on the mouth are best because when pressure is applied the horse will be sensitive to it.

The Seat

The proper seat in the saddle provides the rider and the horse with comfort and security. The seat should be such that it positions the legs for effective use in guiding and controlling the horse. A good seat should provide for effective use of the hands independent of the seat. In other words, an unbalanced seat can cause poor use of the hands on the horse's mouth.

There are three general types of seats which are dependent on the type of horse and saddle you are using. The English varieties are the *hunter* or *forward seat* and the *saddle seat.* The other is the *western seat.* We will be primarily involved with the hunter or forward seat.

Mount the horse and hold and adjust the reins as mentioned above. Adjust your stirrups to the proper length by taking your feet out, allowing your leg to hang down, and raise or lower them until the bottom of the stirrup is at your ankle. Replace your feet making sure the stirrup leathers are flat along the inside of your leg.

A balanced seat is composed of three points: the seat bones and the crotch. The seat is in the middle and lowest part of the saddle and is maintained by rhythm, balance and the grip of the legs. The idea is to keep your body as close to the moving horse as possible through all paces and at all times be independent of the hands.

Inexperienced riders try to maintain their balance by using their hands, which causes jerking and pulling on the horse's mouth. The seat should be maintained by learning to move with the horse and by the use of the pressure applied by the legs.

The main portion of your weight should be in the stirrups. The feet should be into the broadest part of the sole of the foot. If you just put the toe in you cannot support your weight as well. If your foot is in up to the heel of your boot you cannot keep your heel down. You should be able to feel the stretch in the Achilles tendon if your heels are down properly. This prevents the foot from sliding through the stirrup. (These are also good reasons for wearing a heeled shoe or boot that is securely fastened as opposed to a sneaker or loafer.) The weight in the stirrup and the pressure will help to secure your seat and prevent your leg from wobbling around. (See Figure 7-12)

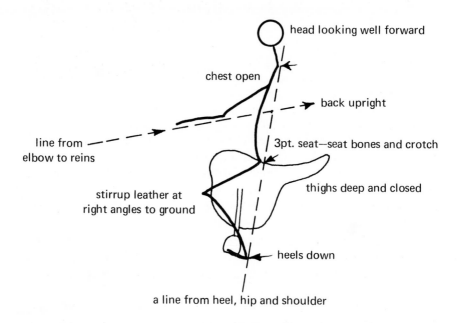

Figure 7-12. The Forward (Hunter) Seat.

Riding at a Walk

After securing the correct hands and seat, you are ready to move. You are now ready to communicate with the horse through movements in your hands and legs. The horse's walk is a four beat gait.

To get the horse to *walk*, apply pressure with the legs. It is not an actual kick. Have a loose rein and allow the horse to walk. Sometimes a clicking noise made with the mouth is an auditory signal to the horse. (See Figure 7-13)

To *stop*, hold the reins firmly and apply pressure with the legs, forcing the horse forward into the bit, thus stopping him. Make sure your hands are far enough forward on the reins so when you pull back you do not have your hands in your lap with no room to pull back.

Practice walking and stopping until you have mastered these signals and then try *backing* your horse. This is done by increasing the pressure on the bit until the horse takes a step backward. Release the pressure and apply it again for another step and continue for about four steps.

To *turn* your horse, pull back with the rein on the side of which you wish to turn. Apply pressure with the same leg just behind the girth. Relax the tension on the opposite rein. Reverse this procedure for a turn to the other side.

Figure 7-13. Horse at a Walk.

When you want to stop your turn, relax the turning hand and leg pressure on that side and become equalized.

Practice these fundamental procedures of tacking, untacking, mounting, dismounting, walking, stopping, backing and turning until you have mastered them and feel confident and ready to change speed to the trot.

Riding at a Trot

When a horse trots, he springs from one pair of diagonal legs to the other. It is a two beat gait.

To get the horse to trot apply more pressure with the legs than was used for the walk and relax the pressure on the bit. (You must always have light pressure on the bit). Lean forward at the hip with a straight back. To stop him from trotting, apply increased pressure on the bit until he responds by walking.

The trot is a rough bouncy gait and to avoid being bounced all over the saddle one must learn to "post." To post you must rise up off the saddle by pressing down in the stirrups when one set of diagonals is off the ground. The seat returns to the saddle as that set of diagonals return to the ground. This is a rhythm that takes time to maintain. It takes practice and trial and error. It might be helpful if you or your instructor counts up one-down two until you have the rhythm. You might have to try again and again, but once you have it you will not forget it. It is like learning to ride a bike or learning to swim. (See Figure 7-14)

Practice going from a walk to a trot and a standstill to a trot. Then practice trotting with a change of direction, going around the

Figure 7-14. Horse at a Trot.

ring to the right and then to the left. Try trotting in a figure eight pattern. When you feel you have mastered trotting in a good balanced seat, good hands, and good control, you are ready to progress to the next gait which is the canter.

Riding at a Canter

The canter is a three beat gait. A horse canters and gallops on either a right or left lead. The lead leg is the fore one which appears ahead of the other during the period of suspension. During the period of suspension all four feet are off the ground. The horse should lead on his left foreleg when circling to the left and on his right foreleg when circling to his right. To put a horse on the left lead when circling to the left, turn his head slightly to the right (thus freeing his left shoulder) and apply pressure, slightly behind the girth, with the right leg. This transfers the weight to the left leg so that the right will start the movement for a left lead. The reverse should be done when circling to the right and the right lead is desired.

To ride at a canter the seat remains in the saddle. The rider leans forward slightly (less than the lean for the trot) in order to keep his balance. The hips rock with the canter of the horse allowing the seat to maintain contact. (See Figure 7-15)

Riding is not a skill that is learned overnight and caution must be taken and attention paid to the safety factors. A hard hat should be worn at all times to protect the head.

Proper attire can be obtained at a later date and should include boots (high top or jodhpur) riding pants, (breeches with high top boots or jodhpur pants with jodhpur boots) a shirt and tie and a riding jacket. The proper attire is called the riding habit and has formal and less formal styles used in showing and hunting.

Figure 7-15. Horse at a Canter.

Once the skills mentioned in this chapter are well mastered the rider is ready to progress to other facets of the sport. These include: trail riding, cross country riding, jumping, fox hunting and showing.

Remember, horsemanship involves everything you can learn about the horse and your relationship to him. Listen to experienced horsemen and learn all you can. Enjoy your new sport.

TERMINOLOGY

Aged—A horse ten years of age or older.

Bay—A brown horse with a black mane and tail and black stockings.

Canter—A gait of moderate speed which has three beats and a moment of suspension. It takes a horse approximately five minutes to cover a mile at a canter.

Chestnut—A reddish brown colored horse which varies in shades from light to dark. The lighter shade is sometimes referred to as a sorrel. Chestnuts usually have white markings.

Cavaletti—A series of low rails.

Colt—A young male horse.

Conformation—The form and build of a horse.

Cross-ties—Two lengths of rope or chain attached to opposite walls or poles which hook to both sides of the horse's halter. The horse can be secured in these to be groomed or worked around.

Dressage—Refers to a rider putting a horse through complex maneuvers with very little visible effort or movement in hands or legs.

Equitation—The art of riding.

Filly—A young female horse up to four years of age.

Foal—A newborn horse. This term does not indicate the sex.

Frog—The tender part of the underside of the horse's hoof which is V-shaped. It is prone to injury when a horse is ridden on hard roads or rocky surfaces.

Gallop—This gait is faster than the canter. A horse can gallop a mile in approximately four minutes.

Gelding—A male horse which has been castrated before reaching maturity. He is generally more passive and more easily handled in the company of other horses than a stallion.

Hacking—Pleasure riding the country usually without jumping.

Hand—A unit of measurement equaling four inches used to determine the height of a horse.

Left-lead—Leading with left leg when circling to the left in a ring at a canter.

Longeing—Working or schooling a horse on a long line attached to the halter. The trainer stands in the center and works the horse in a circle.

Mare—Female horse at the age of five and over.

Martingale—An attachment to either the noseband or the reins which goes down between the front legs and attaches to the girth. It gives added control over the horse and helps to prevent rearing.

Near-side—The left side of the horse.

Off-side—The opposite of the near side or the right side of the horse.

Pelham—A straight bar bit, frequently covered with hard rubber, accompanied with a curb chain.

Posting—A rhythmic movement of rider in coordination with horse at a trot. This is not done in Western riding.

Right-lead—Leading with the right front leg at a canter.

Snaffle—A broken bar bit which applies the least pressure of any bit to the horse's mouth.

Stallion—An adult male horse which can be used for breeding.

Trot—A gait in which there is a moment of suspension as the horse starts to jump from one diagonal to the other. There are two beats to the trot. It takes a horse approximately six and one-half minutes to trot a mile.

Walk—A four beat gait which has no moment of suspension. It takes approximately fifteen minutes to walk a mile.

Weanling—A foal who has been taken from its mother at about six months of age.

BIBLIOGRAPHY

Churchhill, Peter. *Progressive Steps in Riding.* New York: ARCO Publishing Company, Inc., 1964.

Disstan, Harry. *Young Horseman's Handbook.* Virginia: The Jarman Press, 1970. Numbers 1-10.

Friffen, Jeff. *The Book of Horses and Horsemanship.* New York: Bonanza Books, 1963.

Kulesza, S. R. *Modern Riding.* New York: A.S. Barnes and Company, 1970.

Littaver, Vladimir S. *Common Sense Horsemanship.* New York: Van Nostrand Reinhold Company, 1951.

SKIING

BEHAVIORAL OBJECTIVES

1. Prior to the initial ski lesson on a ski slope, the college student will be able to achieve a score of at least 75 per cent on a written examination concerned with the National Skier's Code.
2. The college student will be able to demonstrate a thorough understanding of proper equipment and suitable ski clothing by using such equipment and clothing on the ski slopes.
3. The college student will be able to successfully demonstrate (meet *all* the essential criteria as stated in the chapter) the proper method of carrying skis, putting skis on and holding ski poles.
4. Given a ski slope with normal conditions, the college student will be able to successfully perform (meet *all* the essential criteria as stated in the chapter) the following skiing fundamentals:
   a. Step turn on a flat terrain. The turn must be a 180 degree reversal of direction.
   b. Falling.
   c. Rising after a fall.
   d. Walking and gliding on a level and straight upgrade.
   e. Sidestep up a 15 degree slope.
   f. Herringbone up a 10 degree slope for 50 feet.
   g. Traverse sidestep up a 15 degree slope for 50 feet.
   h. Step turn on a 10 degree slope.
   i. Straight running position down a 10 degree slope for a minimum of 50 feet.
   j. Four linked snowplow turns on a 10 degree slope.
   k. Braking speed for 50 feet on a 10 degree slope using the snowplow.
   l. Four linked stem turns on a slope of not less than 10 degrees.
   m. Kick turn to both the right and the left on the level. The turn must be a 180 degree reversal of direction with the skis finishing parallel.

n. Kick turn right and left on a slope of not less than 10 degrees.
o. Traverse for at least 50 feet going both right and left on a slope of not less than 15 degrees.
p. Four linked stem turns on a slope of not less than 15 degrees.
q. Three long traverses across a 10 degree slope linking the traverses with a stem turn.
r. Controlled sideslipping in two directions down the fall line for 20 feet.
s. Right and left stop on a slope of not less than 15 degrees using the uphill christie.

5. The college student will be able to achieve a score of 75 per cent on a written examination concerned with the history, terminology and analysis of skiing fundamentals.

HISTORY OF SKIING

People have skied for thousands of years—the Finns for at least five thousand. Skis have been found that are over four thousand years old. There is evidence that people hunted on skis as early as the sixteenth century, and in the middle of the eighteenth century the Norwegians used ski troops as part of their army.

It was not until about 1820, however, that skiing finally emerged as a sport. Until this time there is no evidence that skiing was done for sport; skis were used exclusively for transportation. When the Norwegians, who began the first competitive skiing, became enthusiastic about the sport they rapidly spread it throughout the world. Styles and equipment have changed considerably since the inception of skiing as a sport, but the initial enthusiasm has not abated. Indeed, it has continued to increase since skiing first became a recreational activity. In the United States alone, there are 3,500,000 skiers and skiing is one of our fastest growing sports.

NATURE OF SKIING

Skiing is generally considered in the realm of sport these days; very little consideration is given to skiing as a mode of transportation. In America the sport of skiing is usually thought of as competitive or recreational in nature. In this chapter we will consider the recreational aspect of skiing, skiing for fun.

Recreational skiing is a rigorous sport. It is strenuous exercise and requires a great expenditure of energy. To prepare yourself for the demands of skiing you must undertake a conditioning program.

If you wish to ski, and to ski well, you must get in shape and stay in shape.

Pre-skiing conditioning makes skiing not only safer, but also more fun. Because a finely-tuned body is more resistant to injury than a flaccid one, you automatically reduce the possibility of injury when you have conditioned your body well. If your body is physically ready to cope with the special stresses and strains of skiing, you will learn faster and ski better. Your increased endurance through conditioning will permit you to ski longer in a day. Without a certain amount of strength, stamina and agility you will not be able to perform many of the maneuvers involved in skiing. If you are unable to execute these maneuvers satisfactorily, you will deprive yourself of the exhilaration and pride of accomplishment which is so much a part of skiing.

Many exercises will help you to get in shape for skiing. The exercises you elect to perform should stretch, strengthen and relax the muscles in your legs, abdomen, back, shoulders and arms. In addition, the exercises should give your heart and lungs a workout, limber up your joints, increase your stamina, improve your balance and sharpen your reflexes. As a bonus they will help with weight control. Begin your conditioning program at least a month before your initial ski attempt. A short period of basic calisthenics performed daily is superior to an elaborate plan which is followed intermittently. Those muscles used in running and jumping are essentially the same as those used in skiing. Therefore, rope jumping, stationary jumping, sprinting and jogging are especially effective exercises. Skiers find beneficial many of the standard conditioning exercises such as: half knee bends (avoid deep knee bends), sit-ups, toe touches, push-ups, hand stands, head stands and ankle swivels.

A number of exercises have been designed particularly for skiers. One of the most important, the "invisible chair," strengthens your thigh and quadriceps muscles. To sit in the "invisible chair," first place your back flat against the wall. Place your feet 12 to 18 inches from the wall and slide your back down the wall until you are in a sitting position. Your feet should be directly under your knees, which are bent 90 degrees. Your thighs will be parallel to the floor and your lower legs perpendicular to the floor. (See Figure 8-1)

A "tendon stretch" is especially good for women skiers whose tendons are likely to be tight as a result of wearing high heels. Stand facing a wall at a distance of about 12 inches. Your feet should be comfortably spaced. Bend forward from the ankles until you can do a push up against the wall. As this becomes easier, increase the

Figure 8-1. "Invisible Chair."

distance of your feet from the wall until you reach a maximum distance of 36 inches.

If you follow the *Royal Canadian Air Force* program for your age bracket you will be fit for skiing. Several other standard exercising programs are described in the books which are listed in the bibliography. These programs, which describe the exercises in detail and suggest appropriate use, will be helpful to you as you prepare a personalized exercise plan. Your ski instructor will also help you with this pre-skiing phase.

The nature of skiing is such that serious injuries can occur if proper precautions are not taken. One cause of ski injuries is poor physical conditioning. Skiing accidents also result from the failure of some skiers to use good judgment and/or ski courtesy on the slopes. They take the most enticing lift to the top of the mountain without knowing if there is a way down appropriate for their skill. They ski precariously close to other skiers, and to add insult to injury, they do not even bother to shout a word of warning. They barrel down a slope out of control because they overestimate their own ability. As you can see, the careless skier endangers not only himself but others as well. Being courteous and considerate on the slope is a mark of good judgment. Warn a skier if you are going to overtake him and give him a wide berth as you pass. Don't tailgate. If you make a sitz mark in the snow when falling, be sure to fill it in for the sake of those who follow.

It is also good judgment to investigate the trail marking system at a ski area *before* you take a lift up the hill. Learn the meanings of the markings and decide which trails you can ski safely. Evaluate your ability honestly and ski accordingly. Many ski areas now use a standardized marking system, but regardless of the type of system in use, it will indicate with various colored geometric designs the relative difficulty of the trail. If there is any doubt in your mind, any ski instructor or ski patrolman will be happy to assist you.

The *National Ski Patrol System* has helped to devise some "rules of the road" to avoid injuries which stem from lack of courtesy and/or lack of regard for safety rules. Read and follow these common-sense precautions as set forth in the *National Skier's Courtesy Code:*

1. All skiers shall ski under control at all times. Control means in such a manner that a skier can avoid other skiers and objects.
2. When skiing downhill and overtaking another skier, the overtaking skier shall avoid the skier below him.
3. Skiers approaching each other on opposite traverses shall pass to the right of each other.
4. Skiers shall not stop in a location which will obstruct a trail where they are not visible from above, or where they will impede the normal passage of other skiers, either in motion or while loading or unloading ski lifts.
5. A skier entering a trail or slope from a side or intersecting trail shall first check for approaching downhill skiers before proceeding.
6. A standing skier shall check for approaching downhill skiers before starting.
7. When walking or climbing in a ski area, skis should be worn and the ascending skier shall keep to the side of the trail or slope.
8. All skiers shall wear safety straps or other retaining devices to prevent runaway skis.
9. Skiers shall not enter closed areas or trails and shall observe all traffic signs and other regulations as prescribed by the ski area and its ski patrolmen.

Adherence to the above standards of conduct will reduce your chances of being injured and help to make the slopes safer for all skiers.

EQUIPMENT

Use of proper equipment is very important. Faulty equipment, like poor physical conditioning or lack of good judgment, can cause accidents. Equipment chosen specifically for your requirements will make skiing safer, easier and more fun. Ironically, however, one does not know precisely what equipment is best or what he likes most until he has done some skiing. Fortunately this dilemma is solved by the innumerable shops where ski equipment can be rented. It is advisable for beginners to rent good quality boots, skis and poles for their first few outings. It is not advisable to borrow equipment from friends as it is usually either well-worn or ill-fitting. Renting equipment affords you the opportunity to learn more about the many brands of equipment and to determine your particular preferences. It also allows you to determine whether you enjoy the sport sufficiently to invest the considerable amount of money necessary to purchase your own equipment.

Boots, Skis, Poles

Once you begin to purchase your own equipment, start with the basics and purchase them in this order: boots, skis, bindings and poles. Specialty shops will provide you with sound advice on what equipment to purchase. Boots are your most fundamental piece of equipment. It is critical that boots fit properly for they transmit the motion of your legs and feet to your skis. Since it is essentially your feet and legs that control your skis, you want to be sure your transmitting element is A-OK. Boots should fit snugly enough so your heels do not rise up. Your feet should not slide or twist around in the boots, but on the other hand, the boots should not be so tight that they inhibit circulation or prohibit wiggling your toes easily. The sides of the boot must be stiff enough to firmly support your ankles laterally but still allow the ankle to flex forward freely. The sole of the boot should be rigid. The boot should touch your instep, but not press against it. Force your heel completely to the back of the boot before tightening it. Be particular about the fit of the boot. Try on several brands to help you decide which boot fits best. To insure an exact fit when trying on ski boots, wear the socks you intend to wear when skiing. Usually one thin pair of socks worn under one pair of medium thickness (wool or thermal) provides maximum warmth. Most skiers today are buying buckle boots, although some good lace boots are still available. When you think you have found the boots you want, walk around in them for 15 to 20 minutes to determine how they fit. If they still feel all right they are probably a good fit for you.

Like boots, bindings should receive special attention. They not only must secure your boots firmly to your skis through all skiing maneuvers, but they must also release at critical times to avoid your sustaining injury in a fall. Step-in bindings are presently considered the safest type. Your specialty shop can suggest the binding which is most suitable for your body build and level of skiing. Always purchase and attach safety straps before your first skiing attempt. Straps that attach on each side of your boot are recommended. One end of the safety strap is attached to the binding, the other end to your boot. This prevents a runaway ski in the event your ski is released from your binding during a fall. A runaway ski hurtling down the slope can seriously injure other persons, or even vanish into oblivion.

Selection of the proper skis is both important and difficult. Actually there is no one ski awaiting you. There is a myriad of types, brands and models from which to choose, many of which would be satisfactory. Your specialty shop can assist you in narrowing the choices as well as in suggesting an appropriate length. There are numerous opinions on the correct length of skis. As a general rule, however, skis should be from three to eight inches taller than the skier.

Beginners, especially those who are lightweight or not particularly athletic, usually find that skis reaching a few inches above their heads are most satisfactory. Heavier skiers, and those who are in very good physical shape or are extremely well-coordinated, may wish to use skis a bit longer. When considering length, remember that a longer ski generally has more stability than a shorter ski, but the longer ski is also more difficult to turn. Specialty shops have charts which will suggest an appropriate length ski after such factors as your height, weight, age, sex, physical capabilities and skiing experience are considered. Nowadays there is even a computer which, when fed the vital information, can advise you about the best make and model ski you might buy.

Ultimately you must make the decision as to type, brand, model and length you will purchase, but the following guidelines may assist you when an overwhelming number of choices confronts you. If you are heavy for your height, you need a stiff model; if you are average in weight, standard flex is good; and if you are a lightweight, you need a soft, very flexible model. Of the three major types of skis—wood, metal and fiberglass—wood skis are the least expensive and the least durable. Metal skis are the most durable and turn more easily than the wooden ski, but they do not absorb shocks from changes in terrain as well as the two other types. Although not yet perfected, fiberglass skis, and combinations of fiberglass with other materials, possess some of the better qualities of all constructions and seem to be the skis of the future. Usually the more expensive skis are not designed for beginners.

As with skis, there are various opinions concerning the correct length of poles. Again the final decision is yours. After learning the standard limits and experimenting with various lengths, you must decide what you personally prefer. Nearly all skiers prefer pole lengths to be somewhere between waist high and armpit level. Several inches below the armpit is most common for recreational skiers. If you are not certain what length you prefer, buy your poles on the long side and have them cut down gradually by your ski shop until you find your preferred length. Any poles you purchase should be strong yet light, with small, light baskets. Since poles are used for assistance in many maneuvers, they should feel well balanced. Choice of poles is a matter of personal preference, so choose ones which feel right for you.

Clothing

Once the necessities of equipment are accounted for, turn your attention to ski clothing. Again start with the basics; in this case: long underwear (top and bottom), socks, ski pants, sweater, jacket, hat and gloves. Warmth is your primary consideration, but it is possible to combine function with fashion. Fishnet, thermal or 2-ply wool long underwear will keep you snug and warm. Durable pants, preferably water resistant, are a must. Ski pants or denim-like pants are currently most fashionable. A warm (functional), colorful (fashionable) sweater, often worn over a turtle neck shirt is also necessary. Don't forget two pairs of socks, as mentioned earlier. Don't advertise the fact you are a beginner by wearing your socks up and over the legs of your ski pants. They are neither fashionable nor functional that way. Snow accumulates on socks worn over pants. The moisture in the snow is drawn down into the feet of the socks and will make your feet wet and, consequently, cold. An insulated, water repellent parka is necessary on cold days. It should have a hood which tucks into a collar when not needed. The collar should be high enough to cut off the wind if necessary. The parka should also have pockets that are zippered and cuffs that fit snugly at the wrists to shut out cold and snow. To protect your ears, wear a headband or, as most skiers do, a colorful hat. Special ski gloves or mittens should be worn to keep your hands warm and dry. Some prefer mittens because they are warmer, and others prefer gloves because they offer greater freedom of movement. Regardless of which you wear, they should be well insulated and have reinforced palms. The gauntlets should be long, with elastic knit to fit snugly about the wrists to retain heat and keep out snow.

Don't wear scarves or other items that may streak out behind you and become entangled in rope tows or other objects. Be certain that none of your clothing is so tight it restricts circulation. You can count on being cold if it does. For those of you who detest the cold but still want to ski, long silk underwear, socks and liners for gloves are available to wear in addition to your basic layers of clothing. Silk clothing is more expensive, but some say it keeps you warmer than its more conventional counterparts. Regardless of your choice of material for clothing, wear several thin layers rather than one heavy layer. Several thin layers are best for trapping heat and keeping you warm.

The list of accessories is endless. First priority goes to a boot tree for carrying and properly storing your boots. Rubber ski ties to hold your skis together are extremely useful. Goggles are also important. Expensive ones keep the wind and snow out without fogging up. Various interchangeable, colored lenses can be inserted into the goggles to adjust for varying light conditions. It is helpful to have ski wax which can be applied to the bottoms of your skis in certain snow conditions. As you continue to ski, you will discover more and more accessories for skiing which you would like. If you become a real ski enthusiast, you will even want rain gear so neither rain nor sleet will keep you from fun on the slopes.

SKILLS TO BE DEVELOPED

The American Ski Technique

There are a variety of ski techniques and numerous methods for teaching them. The American Ski Technique has been adopted and developed by the Professional Ski Instructors of America to insure competent, uniform and sequential instruction throughout the country. Local terrain and snow conditions cause adaptations in teaching methods, but the same techniques with the same sequential development of skills and standard goals now exist throughout the country. Although other techniques have their merits, we will adhere primarily to the American Ski Technique as interpreted through the writer's personal bias as a ski instructor.

Carrying Skis

Before actually skiing, you must transport your skis and poles to a spot which is convenient to the area where you plan to ski. Don't carry your equipment in outstretched arms like a bundle of uncooperative firewood. First place your poles firmly in the snow to free both your hands. Then stand your skis on their tails with their bottoms together. (See Figure 8-2a) Press the skis together firmly and lift them up until you can grasp them tightly at the tails with one hand. Now shoulder the skis as if carrying a rifle. Grasp the poles at the tops with your free hand. You may use the poles either in cane fashion for balance or place them on your other shoulder to offset the weight of the skis. (See Figure 8-2b) Exercise care when turning around with skis on your shoulder to avoid delivering a swinging *KO blow* to unsuspecting bystanders.

a. lifting ski   b. shouldering ski

Figure 8-2. Carrying Skis.

Putting Skis On

Place your skis side by side, both pointing in the same direction, on a flat area which is close to the intended skiing area. Later, when you need to put your skis on while standing on an incline, you will place your skis at right angles to the *fall line*. (The fall line is the shortest line down a hill.) Before placing your boot in the binding, scrape accumulated snow off your boot soles. Put your downhill ski on first, for it assists in balance and leverage. (When you are on the slope, the downhill ski will be the one nearest to the bottom of the slope.) Center your boot carefully so it points directly ahead. Then put on your uphill ski (the one nearest the top of the slope). Use your poles for balance if necessary; it probably will be. Attach your safety straps securely but not so tightly that they restrict circulation. Be sure to fasten each strap from the outside of the boot to the outside of the ski. If the straps are fastened on the inside the slack in the strap may catch under a ski.

Holding Poles

Hold the shaft of the pole in your left hand with the loop facing you. Place your right hand between the loop and the shaft, with the fingers pointing upward and palm facing the shaft. From this position, slip your right hand up through the loop until you can place your palm on the butt of the grip. In this position you will find your hand directly above the jointure of the loop straps and the grip. Keep the straps under your palm as you slide your right hand down the grip until you can wrap your fingers around the pole grip. The straps are always secured between your hand and the pole grip while the loop rests lazily on your wrist. (See Figure 8-3) Repeat the process with the other pole. Now the loops will hold the poles on your wrists even if you should let go of the grips.

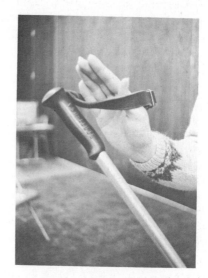

Figure 8-3. Holding Poles.

Becoming Comfortable on Skis

Perform the following exercises on flat ground to gain the feel of your skis. While standing still, alternately raise the tail of one ski and then the other. Next, place all your weight on one ski and raise the other ski. Notice how the tip of the raised ski drops. You must always raise the tip of the ski when lifting a ski to compensate for the weight of the front of the ski. Repeat the lifting of each ski until the skis begin to feel like a natural extension of your feet. Repeat this exercise periodically to help maintain a feel for the unbalanced ski tip. Now raise your right ski and turn the tip to the left and then the right. Repeat this with your left ski. When you can do this with ease, step sideways with your right ski and then step back again. Step sideways with the left ski, too. Now you should feel comfortable on your skis and able to proceed to slightly more advanced motions.

Step Turn

Step turns are used to change direction on relatively flat terrain. To visualize the turn, imagine your skis as hands of a clock which will move around the face of the clock. To begin, place your feet together and parallel. Transfer all your weight to one ski (this is now the weighted ski), keep the tails together, and move the tip of the unweighted ski out about 12 inches. (See Figure 8-4a) Your skis now form a "V". Shift your weight to the ski you just moved and pivot the other ski up to the weighted ski, keeping the tails close together. Continue lifting each ski alternately as you transfer your weight and pivot around the tails in order to effect a change of direction. You can make a complete 360 degree turn in this fashion. Practice turning both clockwise and counter clockwise.

An alternate method is to keep the tips in place while separating only the tails. Keep the tip of the ski on the snow and move the tail of the ski about a foot away from the other tail. You will form an inverted "V". (See Figure 8-4b) As in the previous maneuver, place all your weight on the stationary ski to permit you to swing the unweighted ski in parallel to the stationary one. Continue alternating the transfer of weight and the separation of the skis until you have made a complete circle. Practice moving in both directions.

a. stationary tail   b. stationary tip

Figure 8-4. Step Turn.

Later on in your skiing you can even use the step turn on a slight incline. If facing downhill, use the stationary tip method and open the tails to change direction. Plant your poles on the outsides of your skis and towards the tips to keep from sliding forward. If facing uphill, open the tips and pivot around the tails. Keep a pole on either side of you and back toward the tails to prevent sliding back. Practice first on flat terrain. Keep relaxed. The pattern you make should resemble a large fan.

Falling and Rising

Though unintended, falls do occur in skiing. Falling correctly, like skiing properly, is a learned skill. You can practice a safe way to fall and also the easiest way to regain your feet (rising). When your balance cannot be restored and a fall is inevitable, **relax** and follow these suggestions. Don't fight your fall once it is impossible to regain your balance. Accept your plight and concentrate on falling safely. Relax! Fall backwards and to the side in a sitting position so your hip or seat can bear the brunt of the fall. Keep your knees and feet together to avoid crossing the skis or exerting pressure against the legs. Avoid setting up resistance by digging a knee into the snow, letting a leg twist underneath you as you go down or extending your arms to break the fall. If possible, kick both legs out free of the snow. To make a good fall, squat, sit and kick. Tense, taut muscles also offer more resistance and make injury more likely, so relax. When and if you fall, concentrate on falling backwards and to the side in a controlled, skillful fall.

After falling, dust yourself off (laugh at yourself with your friends) and prepare to stand up. You may need to disentangle your skis. Sometimes you may even have to roll over on your back and raise your legs in the air to untangle them. Place your skis downhill from you, perpendicular to the fall line. Don't try to get up when your skis are uphill from you because you are working against gravity. Placing your skis across the fall line will keep them from slipping down the hill, but you must get them below you first. Remove the ski poles from your wrists. Draw your knees up tightly and tuck your boots well up under and as close as possible to your hips. (See Figure 8-5a)

When your feet are close to your hips your weight will be directly over your feet as you get up. This will facilitate your rising. Keep your skis on their uphill edges to prevent them from sliding downhill. Plant the tips of both poles in the snow beside your uphill hip. Place your uphill hand on the shafts, near the baskets. Hold the ends of the grips, or as far up as you can reach, with the other hand. (See Figure 8-5b)

With a hard thrust on your poles, push yourself up, rolling your weight over your skis as soon as you can. Once your weight is over

a. preparatory position   b. rising

Figure 8-5. Rising.

your skis you can use the strength of your legs to help boost you. As you become more upright, slide your uphill hand up the poles. Some skiers prefer, after they have tucked their feet up under their hips, to hold their poles in the downhill hand and use the uphill fist to push against the snow and right themselves. Which ever method you employ, the secret is to bunch yourself as closely over your feet as possible. Then give a strong upward push with your uphill arm. Once you have begun to rise, push up with your legs too. Keep your skis edged into the hill throughout the rising process.

Walking on Skis

The body motions for walking on skis are similar to those in regular walking. Just move as if you were walking down the street. Keep your skis on the snow and slide one ski forward. Transfer your weight to the forward ski and bring the other ski up a comfortable distance ahead of the first ski. Transfer your weight again to the forward ski and repeat the procedure as you slide each ski forward alternately. Use your poles for balance. Slant them back and plant them close to your boots. As in normal walking, poles and arms move naturally, with the left pole advancing with the right ski and the right pole advancing with the left ski. Keep your weight forward and your knees bent as you step. (See Figure 8-6) Slide the skis rather than lift them. Practice on flat terrain. When you can walk using your poles, walk without using them.

Sliding

Sliding is like walking but covers distance more rapidly. The same procedure is followed except that the poles are used to propel the skier. As the pole passes the body, apply a strong thrust to the pole to push yourself forward in a gliding fashion. Practice this maneuver on flat terrain or a slight downgrade that has a natural runout.

Figure 8-6. Walking.

Climbing

The three basic ways of climbing up a slope are: *the side-step, the diagonal sidestep* and *the herringbone.*

Sidestep. To perform the simplest maneuver, the sidestep, begin with your skis parallel, all your weight on your downhill ski and your skis perpendicular to the fall line. Hold your poles on either side of you and use them for balance. Plant your uphill pole in line with your body at arm's length. Lift the uphill ski off the snow and place it about 12 inches directly up the slope and parallel to your downhill ski. (See Figure 8-7) Transfer your

Figure 8-7. Sidestepping.

weight to your uphill ski and then bring your downhill ski up to and parallel with the uphill ski. Keep your weight on the uphill edges of your skis to prevent sliding. Follow this by re-planting your uphill

pole at arm's length up the hill. Transfer your weight to your downhill ski and continue the process.

Remember to raise your tips as you step uphill. Don't be timid
when placing your ski uphill—tramp down firmly on the uphill edge
with a flexed knee. If you tend to slide forward or backward, you
probably are not keeping your skis perpendicular to the ever-present
fall line. If your skis tend to slip sideways downhill, apply more
edging by pushing your well-bent knees farther in toward the hill. If
your tails and/or tips cross, you are not raising and moving your skis
evenly. Lift the ski and the leg from your hip, not your ankle, and
remember to compensate for a heavier tip than tail.

In sidestepping, haste makes waste. Take small deliberate steps.
The sidestep can be utilized to ascend any hill. It is most useful,
however, on short, steep slopes. Practice sidestepping on a gentle
incline facing first in one direction and then in the other to be sure
that you are equally facile with either right or left side uphill. Sidestep back down the incline until such time as you know how to
snowplow down under control.

Diagonal Sidestep. If you wish to make a long climb, the diagonal
or traverse sidestep is less tiring than the sidestep. Sidestepping diagonally is merely a combination of sidestepping and walking. To move
forward and uphill simultaneously, you simply move the skis forward
as you lift them uphill. To start, lift the uphill ski up and forward,
setting it down on its uphill edge. Next, bring the downhill ski up
and ahead of the uphill ski. In this way you not only climb the hill
but proceed across it. Maintain a position where your body is centered over the skis with your knees flexed and pressed toward the
slope. Take comfortable steps and use your poles for support and
forward thrust. Look ahead, but glance uphill frequently in order to
avoid interfering with descending skiers.

The Herringbone. The herringbone is used primarily for making a
direct, short ascent; it is taxing for long distances. Face uphill on a
slight incline and place both poles behind you on the outsides of
your skis. Keeping the tails of your skis together, open the tips to
form a "V". With your weight on the inside edge of one ski, take a
comfortable step uphill and outward with the other, and then alternate. Plant each ski diagonally and decisively on its inside edge. Keep
both knees flexed and pressed inward. Stay on your inside edges and
push behind you on your poles to keep you from slipping back down
the incline. As you step forward, step outward a sufficient distance
to avoid setting the tail of one ski on the tail of the other. (See Figure
8-8)

Always maintain a "V" position while climbing; widen the "V"

Figure 8-8. Herringbone.

and increase the edging as the slope becomes steeper. Your poles are used behind you for balance and additional support while you are climbing. Move them alternately as you step, right pole with left leg, left pole with right leg. As the slope becomes steeper, place your hands over the tops of the pole grips to give added reach and thrust. As you alternately step each ski uphill in the "V" position, you will form a herringbone pattern. Most skiers develop a preference for one particular type of climbing, but if they are doing extensive climbing they vary the routine by alternating the herringbone with side-stepping and diagonal sidestepping.

Step Turn on a Hill

Once you have climbed up a slope you will want to be able to step around into the fall line in preparation for a run down the hill. The skis are stepped around in the same manner as on flat terrain, but the arms and poles play a vital role by acting as brakes to prevent your sliding prematurely downhill as you step around.

Begin by standing perpendicular to the fall line. Bend slightly at the waist and extend arms and poles as far as possible downhill. Plant both poles below you approximately in line with the tips of your ski boots and about shoulder width apart. Place your palms on the butts of the poles and lock your elbows to make an unbroken line from the pole tips to your shoulders. (See Figure 8-9a) Consider the poles as extensions of your arms and lean on them heavily. This allows all your body weight to be supported on the poles and makes it possible for you to step around under control. As you begin to step, maintain your weight on your poles constantly to avoid premature sliding of your skis.

Step turn your skis until they point downhill through your poles. (See Figure 8-9b) When you are ready to proceed downhill, let the skis slide forward and lift the poles from the snow as you pass them.

a. pole position   b. completed step turn

Figure 8-9. Step Turn.

Straight Running

Once you can correctly ascend a hill and position yourself for the descent, you will want to be able to ski down safely. To descend a slope in the correct running position requires the coordination of many parts of your body. Your skis should be flat, close together and pointed straight ahead with your weight distributed equally on each ski. Either ski may be slightly advanced for added stability. Flex your ankles and press them forward steadily against your boot tops. Like the ankles, your knees are flexed and pressed forward, but should remain flexible enough to act as shock absorbers when encountering irregularities of terrain. If you stand erect over your skis and then kneel, you will be in the correct position. Bend forward slightly from the waist without sticking out your derriere. Always keep your body perpendicular to your skis. Don't lean backwards. Your upper arms hang naturally with elbows flexed. The forearms and hands are held forward, hip high and off the body. Poles are held parallel, up the slope and off the snow. It will help you to assume the correct positioning of your hands and poles if you imagine you are holding the large steering wheel of a bus. To attain the correct forward flexing of the knees and ankles, press them forward as if you were going to kneel down in front of your boots. Don't bend your knees as if you were about to sit down in a chair—this throws your weight back on your ski tails where you

Figure 8-10. Straight Running Position.

don't want it. Pressing the knees and ankles forward keeps your weight over the front part of your skis. (See Figure 8-10)

You will want to practice straight running on a gentle slope where a flat runout at the bottom causes a natural stop. To position yourself for a run down the hill, step turn up the hill into the fall line of the slope. Before releasing your poles, be sure your knees and ankles are pressed forward, your weight is forward and your body is relaxed. (Relaxing isn't easy at first when attempting to carry out all the details of the correct running position, but it will come.) As your proficiency increases, run over slight bumps—swallow the bumps by bending your knees as you go over them—and ride under poles which have been placed together to form an arch. When you can do this, raise the tail of one ski slightly and try to ski on one ski and then the other.

Straight Snowplow

The snowplow is a critical fundamental in skiing which should be diligently practiced. It is the first and most basic method you will learn for controlling the speed of descent, for stopping and for turning. Practice assuming the snowplow position on flat terrain before attempting it on the slope. Standing on the flat, place your skis pointing directly downhill in the fall line. Displace the tails of the skis at equal angles from the fall line to form a wide inverted "V" position. Keep the tips together but not touching. Distribute your weight equally on both skis. Keep your center of gravity ahead of the center of your skis by pressing your knees and ankles forward. Press them inward, also, which will force your skis onto their inside edges. The running surfaces of your skis should be at right angles to your lower legs.

The knees should point towards the tips of the skis and be pressed forward farther than in straight running. The hands are held as in straight running. (See Figure 8-11) Your braking effect, or control, is governed by both the amount of edging and the angle of your snowplow. The greater the angle of your plow, and the more you edge your skis, the slower you will move. To increase the angle of the plow, push your heels out. The tails should be spread apart approximately the length of your ski pole. To provide more edge, press your knees and ankles forward and slightly inward. When you push your heels outward or ankles inward, be careful to avoid a bowlegged or knock-kneed position for this causes loss of control. Imagine yourself straddling a plump horse in order to maintain the correct leg spread. Remember to press the knees and ankles forward as if kneeling. Don't bend your knees and let your weight drop back as if you were sitting! When descending a slope you can decrease speed or come to a complete halt by forcing a wide "V" and edging hard.

Figure 8-11. Straight Snowplow.

Remember to keep your upper body in the straight running position while the knees and ankles are flexed well forward to maintain your weight on the front of the skis. If you are having trouble pushing your heels out, you probably have too much weight on the tails of your skis. Press your weight forward from your knees and ankles while you push out the tails to correct this. If your skis turn out of the fall line, you have more weight on one ski than the other. Distribute your weight equally on each ski.

After practicing the correct position on flat terrain, try hopping from the straight running position into the straight snowplow position. To do this, sink down and forward by bending hard at the knees and ankles. As you hop up and forward from this position your ski tails will be unweighted and you can easily push them out into the snowplow position. Work at displacing the tails at equal angles to the fall line. As you sink down and hop up, always include a forward motion as well, for if you allow your body to lean back you will not be able to unweight the tails.

Now you are ready to snowplow down a hill. Climb up an incline and use the step turn to turn your skis facing downhill. Assume the snowplow position and lift your poles from the snow when you are ready to snowplow down the hill. When you have lifted your poles immediately reposition them in the straight running position. As you gain confidence, experiment by increasing and decreasing the angle of your plow. Increase and decrease the amount of edging by rolling your ankles in and out. With practice you will be able to descend many slopes safely at a pace suitable to your ability.

Straight Running with Snowplow

This combination of running and plowing enables you to practice both straight running and control of speed. Start practicing on a long gentle slope with a runout at the bottom. Begin in a straight running position. When you gain a little speed, lower your body quickly by pressing your knees and ankles forward. This *down-unweighting* will release the weight from the tails of your skis, enabling you to push out the tails into a snowplow position. To control your speed, bend your ankles and knees inward. This causes your edges to bite into the snow—thereby slowing you. After decreasing your speed, release the edges and flatten the skis by rising somewhat from your knees and ankles (never straighten them completely). As your skis flatten out, let them run parallel again, increasing speed in the process. Assume the straight running position. To decrease your speed again, go into the snowplow by down-unweighting, pushing your heels out and edging. Repeat this exercise several times, alternating straight running with the snowplow. As you approach the end of each run, come to a complete stop by using the snowplow. Keep your hands hip high and your poles straight back as you come to a stop. Bend your knees forward but don't arch your back—which will cause your own tail to stick out. Keep your back straight.

When you can displace your tails easily by using the down-unweighting method, try the hopping or up-unweighting you used earlier on the flat. To make the transition from straight running to the snowplow, sink down and then hop up to spread the tails into a snowplow. As you hop up, the weight will be taken off the tails of the skis, which will make it easy to displace them. It is quite important to sink down and forward and up and forward. Remember that your skis are moving forward as you sink down and spring up. If you do not compensate for this by incorporating forward movement, your relative position to the center of the skis will change, and this will place the weight on the tails of the skis. Substitute up-weighting for down-unweighting throughout your run as you alternate straight running with the snowplow. As before, come to a complete stop at the end of each run. Work at developing a smooth, controlled transition from the straight running to the snowplow and back again. Attempt to attain a rhythmical displacement of the tails. Remember that your skis will pick up speed when they are flat and decrease in speed when they are edged. Although either method of unweighting is satisfactory, practice them both alternately to make advanced skiing easier.

Snowplow Turns

The snowplow turn is used to change direction when in the snowplow position and is not difficult to learn. In fact, some of you inadvertently performed a turn when you were learning to snowplow and did not distribute your weight equally on both skis. Practice the moves necessary in the snowplow turn while standing on flat terrain before attempting it on the slope.

Begin in the snowplow position with weight equally distributed on both skis, tips together, tails out, ankles and knees pressed forward and hands off the body held forward and hip high. To make a turn, simply put your weight against the ski that is pointed in the direction you want to go. For instance, to turn to the left, place your weight against the right ski since it is pointing towards the left and you will turn to the left. To turn to the right, shift your weight over against the left ski. Several motions must be followed in order to complete a smooth turn. To initiate a turn, place almost all your weight on one ski or another. The correct way to weight a ski is to lean out over that ski while you swivel and bend slightly at the waist, as if bowing to the weighted ski. Keep the upper body nearly erect. (The weighted ski is now referred to as the outside or turning ski.) This bowing motion will cause your outside shoulder to turn back slightly. (See Figure 8-12) The *outside* shoulder is turned *back* to help maintain weight on the outside ski and to provide stability throughout the turn. Angling out over the turning ski may go against your instinct for self-preservation, but persist, lean out, and you will learn to make a smooth turn. Learn it now; you will progress to parallel skiing much faster.

When you make a turn, your shoulders, arms and hands should work as a unit. Consequently your hands remain in the same position relative to the shoulders and arms as in the straight running position. When weighting the turning ski, press your outside knee forward firmly, and edge it in slightly. The other knee is also flexed forward, but not so far. Don't try to force or

Figure 8-12. Snowplow Turn.

kick your skis around. Be patient! Weighting a ski properly is what makes it turn. Weight and wait! If you press your outside knee forward, angle your upper body out over the turning ski and just remain in this position, your weighted ski will make a smooth, sweeping turn. After you have practiced the weight transfer and a moderate bowing or angulating on the flat, use a gentle slope to practice making turns to the left and to the right. Begin from a straight snowplow down the fall line first and then try it starting from a straight running position. When you shift to the snowplow position, be sure each ski tail is an equal distance from the fall line.

Linked Snowplow Turns

Once you have mastered the snowplow turn to either side, you can begin linking them together, one after another in a series of turns. Let's begin with a turn to the left. Weight the right ski by pressing the right knee forward and angling your upper body out over the turning ski. At the completion of this left turn, transfer your weight to the left ski by pressing the left knee forward and angling out over the left ski. Now you will glide smoothly to the right. The end of the left turn becomes the beginning of the right turn and the completion of your right turn will be the initial phase of your left turn. Keep both knees bent.

The tips of your skis should be close together but not touching. Once you have mastered the use of your legs in this turn, check your shoulders and hands again. Your downhill shoulder and hand should not be held ahead of your inside shoulder and hand.

When learning linked snowplow turns, novices tend to lean into the turn instead of away from it. You must learn to angulate or lean toward the outside of the turn rather than lean into it. Remember to angulate by bowing slightly toward the weighted ski and allowing the outside shoulder to be turned back slightly. Even when completing the turn, continue to angulate so your head and shoulders face downhill. Think of leading the turn with your inside shoulder while your outside shoulder trails. Remember, too, that your hands, arms and shoulders work as a unit as in individual snowplow turns.

If your skis won't turn smoothly you may not be weighting the outside ski sufficiently. Angulate and press the outside knee forward. You may have an uneven plow. Adjust it. Or you may be sitting back and forcing weight on the tails of your skis. Remember that if your weight is on the tails they cannot turn properly. To remedy this, be sure your ankles are pressing hard against the fronts of your boots and that your body is perpendicular to your skis. Don't forget—don't force your skis to turn. Weight the skis properly and they will turn of their own volition.

To practice linked snowplow turns, it is fun to ski through ski poles or slalom flags which you have set up in a fairly straight line about 15 to 20 feet apart. (Move them closer as you become more proficient.) Weave in and out between the poles while maintaining good control. Work at making smooth, rhythmical turns. You will notice that you must plan ahead; turns take time. Look ahead and decide where you are going to make your turn. Then mentally prepare for it in advance so you can make a controlled, unhurried turn just where you wish. (When you can make controlled, even turns, add a little excitement to your practice by running the course without the poles.)

To assist yourself in establishing correct body position, hold both poles in your hands, crosswise in front of you, one hand at either end of the shafts, palms up, and arms held forward in the normal position. While making turns, lean out over the weighted ski; without altering the hand and arm position in relation to the shoulder, draw back your outside shoulder until the poles are nearly parallel to the weighted ski. This exaggerated angulation should help you angulate moderately when holding poles normally as well as provide you with a visual clue if your outside shoulder starts sneaking forward.

Skating

Skating is a means of covering distance faster than sliding and an effective way to change direction. Skating assists in learning weight shifting as well as in improving your balance. You will gain a keener sense of edge control. Most of all, it's fun. Skating is similar to the herringbone in that skis are stepped out diagonally and alternately. To begin skating, push off from one ski (your thrusting or power ski) which is edged inward. The poles are held behind for balance and may be used to supply additional thrust. To produce forward movement, the advanced ski slides forward obliquely as you transfer your weight to it. The forward ski is set down in a relatively flat position and then rolled to its inside edge as it becomes the thrusting ski. The forward or advanced ski is known as the gliding ski. Move the power ski and gliding ski alternately, transferring your weight as you do so.

To gain greater power and speed, bend forward at the waist to keep your head and body low. Also, bend the power leg considerably as you put your weight on it and thrust off from the inside edge onto the gliding ski. Pushing with your poles, palms on the butts, will give you still greater power and momentum. Utilize the momentum gained from the leg and pole thrust to glide momentarily on your advanced ski. When you are competent on level terrain, try skating down a very gentle incline. Be sure to raise the tip of the sliding ski and point it outward. Keep your knees flexed forward. Pick the rear ski up so it does not catch an edge as it comes forward. When you are quite proficient, you will find that you can skate *up* some inclines (a la jet-propelled herringbone).

Kick Turns

Kick turns are used for changing or reversing direction on the flat or on a slope. Practice first on the flat. As you gain proficiency and confidence, make kick turns on steeper and steeper inclines. Place your skis perpendicular to the fall line. Turn your upper body downhill and plant both poles at least shoulder width apart behind your uphill ski. Lean on your poles and put all your weight on the uphill ski. As you slide the unweighted downhill ski forward, swing it into an upright position, which will allow you to set this downhill ski on its tail beside the tip of the uphill ski. Lift from the hip joint to get the necessary high kick needed to stand the ski on end. Your downhill ski is now pointing straight toward the sky. (See Figure 8-13) To extricate yourself from this extraordinary position, use your poles for balance and transfer your weight to the turned ski. Then bring your uphill ski around and place it parallel to the other ski. When both skis are pointing in the same direction, bring your poles around to the usual position. You have now completed a reversal of direction of approximately 180 degrees. This kick turn can be performed on virtually any slope, provided you begin with your skis firmly planted across the fall line and continue to maintain this relation to the fall line as you reposition each ski.

Figure 8-13. Kickturn.

Traverse

A traverse is used to move forward across a slope at any angle to the fall line. A shallow traverse is performed at nearly 90 degrees to the fall line, while a steep traverse is almost in the fall line. It is extremely important to develop a good traverse; it is the basis for any maneuver in advanced skiing where the skis are parallel. Practice assuming the traverse position on the flat before traversing on a hill. In the traverse, the uphill ski, boot, knee, hip, shoulder and hand are slightly ahead. Everything uphill is slightly advanced; even your uphill ear is ahead! Keep the skis parallel and as close as possible. The uphill ski is advanced about one-third of a boot length. Ankles, knees and hips are bent forward. The uphill knee leads, but both knees are held together and press into the hill as well as forward. Your hands are held to the sides of the body and slightly ahead. Neither your hands nor your arms touch your body. Since your hands and arms have moved as a single unit as your uphill shoulder advanced, your poles will still be parallel and now point slightly uphill. Don't watch your skis. Face slightly downhill but watch in the direction you are traveling. The angle of your skis, boots, knees, hips and shoulders should all be the same. Although your weight is forward, your body position is still upright and approximately perpendicular to your skis. Above all else, keep your weight mainly on the downhill ski. (See Figure 8-14)

Speed in a traverse is controlled by the angle of the traverse. The more you point your skis downhill, the faster they will travel. Make only shallow traverses at first and gradually work into steeper traverses as you learn control.

Control in a traverse is supplied by your weight placement and the edges of your skis. Angulation is the term used to de-

Figure 8-14. Traverse.

scribe the positioning necessary to produce correct weight placement and edge control in either turning or traversing. To angulate, bend slightly at the waist and lean out over the downhill ski. (Bow to the downhill ski.) This position maintains weight on the downhill ski. As the upper body is angled outward it will face somewhat downhill. Edge the skis by pressing the ankles, knees and hips into the hill. This simultaneous angling outward of the upper body and pressing into the hill with the knees and hips forms a *comma position*. Use this "comma" position *(angulation)* to keep your weight on the downhill ski and to control your edges. In this way you can control your traverse.

The comma position may seem awkward at first. You need not practice it, however, only on your skis. You may want to practice positioning yourself in the "comma" in your room, waiting in lines or even at parties as a conversation piece. Regardless of where you practice it, keep at it so it begins to feel natural. To simulate the hip movement involved in angulation, imagine that your hands are full of packages and you want to push a door shut with your hip. You must tilt your hips forward and to the side to push the door. This angling of the hips closely resembles the angling of the hips into the hill which is necessary in angulation. Work hard to master the traverse position for it is a vital aspect of good skiing.

Practice traversing on wide slopes. Most skiers tend to prefer one direction to the other, so don't neglect to practice traversing in both directions. Look back at your track. It should be straight and narrow. (The difficult road!) There should be no slipping or sliding down the hill. If you are slipping, angulate more to acquire greater edge control for it prevents slipping. Adjust your edge action to the angle of the slope. The steeper the slope, the more edge action you need. For more edge action, press your hips, knees and ankles farther into the hill. The more you press into the hill with your lower body, however, the more you must counterbalance this action by leaning outward with the upper body. Steep hills tend to intimidate skiers; they instinctively lean in with their upper body. Don't forget: the steeper the hill, the more you must lean out, for the greater the angulation or comma position, the greater the edge action. Leaning downhill with your upper body seems contrary to your instincts, but actually it gives more stability and control since it forces more weight on the downhill ski, and makes greater edging possible. To overcome your apprehensions about leaning downhill, remind yourself that leaning out with your upper body is merely offsetting the tilting in of the lower body, thereby establishing balance impossible to achieve by leaning into the hill.

As in straight running, your flexed knees act as shock absorbers in a traverse. Bend your knees more as the terrain becomes rougher. Pay careful attention to your downhill leg. Many novices tend to stiffen it. Relax, and bend both knees forward. Bobbing up and down as you traverse helps to relax you as well as to flex your knees properly.

To practice angulation and the proper weight placement, try the following exercise. As you traverse the hill, raise the tail of your uphill ski the height of your calf. Allow the tip of your uphill ski to ride beside your downhill ski. If you angulate correctly, you can hold this position across the hill without losing your balance or having your skis slip downhill. Practice this one-footed traverse in both directions. As you practice, your "comma" position will improve and should begin to feel more natural. Your balance will also improve considerably. To end your traverse, step uphill with a few skating steps. Do this by stepping off the edged downhill ski onto the edged uphill ski. Keep the uphill ski slightly advanced and pointed slightly uphill. After stepping onto the uphill ski, bring the downhill ski up beside the uphill ski. After repeating this several times you will come to a smooth halt.

Stem Turn

Stem turns are used to link traverses together while proceeding at a slow speed. It is actually a combination of snowplow turns and traverses. It is quite important to practice individual phases of the stem turn before attempting the complete turn while moving on a slope.

The entire execution of the stem turn will be described first; this overview will show the relation of one phase to another so you will understand the continuity of action. Read the description in its entirety; then practice phase by phase.

Prepare for the stem turn by beginning a shallow traverse in the correct traverse position. Maintain most of your weight on the downhill ski. Stem (that is, step) the uphill ski tail out and up the hill, keeping the tip beside the downhill ski. This position is quite similar to the snowplow with the tips close together and tails out. The stem turn forms an asymmetrical "V" position, however, since the tails are not displaced at equal angles. Press forward with your knees. Prepare for the turn by drawing your upper body and uphill (outside) shoulder back slightly. To do this, turn the upper body toward the stemmed (uphill, outside ski). To effect the turn, gradually weight the stemmed ski by pressing your outside knee forward and simultaneously angling out over the stemmed ski. Your outside (uphill) shoulder will be lowered slightly as a consequence of angling out and sinking forward on

Figure 8-15. Preparatory Position for Stem Turn.

your outside knee. (See Figure 8-15) At this instant you are disobeying the cardinal rules of keeping your weight on the downhill ski and keeping your downhill shoulder back. This fleeting disobedience is permissible, however, for as you turn your upper body back, you are gathering power for the turn. You are also placing yourself and your weight in the correct position for the forthcoming traverse in a new direction. Hold this position until the completion of the turn, and be careful to keep the inside ski flat to prevent dragging it on its edge. Angulate! Don't let your outside shoulder sneak around on you. As you finish the turn, assume the traverse in the new direction by raising the body slightly and weighting the downhill ski completely to allow the uphill ski to slide in parallel to the downhill ski. Make turns to both sides, always initiating and completing the turns with a traverse.

Now that the stem turn has been described in its entirety, you can begin to practice it in phases. Practice the stemming motion first. Assume a traverse posture while in a stationary position. Now stem the uphill ski; displace the tail and keep the tip beside the downhill ski. When the uphill ski is stemmed, it should remain flat until weight is transferred from the downhill ski (at which time the weight transfer and the forward pressure of the knee will cause the ski to be edged). For practice, bring the unweighted stemmed ski back parallel to the downhill ski and resume the traverse position. A slight lifting of the tail of the uphill ski may be necessary when stemming it or returning it to the traverse position. Do this several times until the shift can be made with ease.

Next you should practice turning the upper body into the preparatory position. After you stem your ski, turn your upper body toward the stemmed ski and angle out over it. Press your outside (uphill) knee well forward as you weight the outside (uphill, stemmed) ski. Return to your starting position by transfering your weight to the downhill ski as you assume the traverse position again. Practice the preliminary phases of the turn in both directions and you will then be ready to practice them while moving, but without actually making the turn. Maintain a shallow traverse at all times to control your speed. Follow the exact sequential pattern as described for the stationary exercises. When you can correctly stem, angulate momentarily, and return to a traverse position (with either right or left ski uphill), you are ready to try a stem turn.

When you implement these motions on your moving skis, don't hurry the turn. Follow the sequence of actions you practiced, but continue to angulate until the weighted ski slowly and smoothly slides around. If your ski does not seem to be turning, angulate more and press down harder on your outside ski. Just weight and wait! Do not maintain the snowplow position after the completion of the turn. Notice that when you complete a stem turn on moving skis, you will have reversed your direction. Assume the proper traverse position for this new direction as soon as possible and try each time you practice to assume it sooner than before.

At first, practice on a wide, gentle slope and use a shallow traverse. Once you can smoothly execute complete single turns in both directions, try to link them one after another in serpentine fashion as you did with snowplow turns. Work at making smooth, continuous weight transfers. Be sure to make definite traverses between turns. Rise up somewhat as you complete the turn and go into a traverse; sink down and forward decidedly on the outside knee as you initiate a turn. When you can perform smooth linked stem turns on a slope of 20 degrees you can consider yourself a beginning intermediate skier.

Sideslipping

Sideslipping can be used in descending a steep hill at a slow, controlled rate. Practice in sideslipping will provide invaluable practice in edge control, an essential ingredient of advanced skiing. Sideslipping is performed while in the traverse position, but the skis slide primarily sideways on the running surfaces rather than running forward on the edges. Practice flattening your skis and re-edging them by standing in a traverse position on an incline. Come up to release the edges; sink down to set the edges. When you can release and set your edges at will, you are ready to try sideslipping. From a stationary traverse position initiate the sideslip with an up motion. This decreases your angulation, thereby flattening the skis and releasing the edges from their hold on the slope. Allow your skis to slip several inches down the slope. The rate of sideslipping is controlled by moving the knees and ankles inward or outward. As the knees and ankles are leaned into the hill, the edges are applied; as the knees and ankles are tilted away from the hill, the skis are flattened, which in turn releases the edges. The flatter your skis are to the slope, the more they will slip down the hill. The more edge you use, the less your skis will slip. To stop the slide completely, press your knees into the hill and simultaneously sink down sharply in the "comma" position. By moving the tips downhill you can initiate a slide that moves forward as well as down.

When sideslipping, keep your skis, feet, ankles and knees close together—working as a unit. You may want to push slightly from uphill with your poles to start your skis sliding. If your skis separate as you slip downhill, you probably are not maintaining the correct traverse position. Correct your position by angulating. This will get your weight off the uphill ski and onto the downhill ski. If you do not flatten your skis sufficiently they will not slip. If you flatten them too much your downhill edges will catch and throw you off balance. The ideal place to practice is a hard-packed slope with a slightly convex surface. The slope should be a bit steeper than what you have been practicing on thus far. If you practice on a concave surface it will make sideslipping difficult because the tips and tails are likely to catch. Practice sideslipping forward and straight down. Practice on both your left and right sides.

Uphill Christie

Uphill christies can be thought of in several ways. They are an extension of the forward sideslip; they offer a way to stop when traversing, and they introduce you to the edging and timing necessary in the finish of a stem christie (a turn in which the skis are parallel through most of the turn).

To begin, start across the slope in a traverse. As you proceed across the hill, initiate the christie with a rhythmical down-forward motion, up-forward motion which unweights the skis and starts them skidding downhill. The down-forward, up-forward motion is emphasized so your body weight keeps up with the continued forward progress of your skis as you sink down and come up. As the skis start to skid, sink down again and angulate. This edges your skis again, which, in turn, holds your skis in their new direction—uphill. You will come to a gradual stop (it's a way to stop, remember?) since you will gradually lose momentum when skiing uphill. Don't sit back or straighten up in relief as you begin to stop. Maintain angulation and make your edges bite into the snow until you have come to a very definite stop. Otherwise, your skis will separate or skid out of the turn. Accentuate the kneeling down position as you come to a stop. Notice that the lower you kneel, the sharper your turn uphill and the more quickly you stop. Throughout this maneuver your upper body must remain in the correct traverse position. Your skis should remain together throughout the turn and your weight on the downhill ski. To check this, raise the tail of your uphill ski as you are finishing the christie.

If you have difficulty maintaining a traverse position in the uphill christie, try this exercise to keep your upper body in the correct position. Hold your poles horizontally in your hands, palms up. Keep the poles about waist high and close to your body as you start a normal traverse. Just before you start the uphill christie, push your poles farther out to the downhill side. Hold the poles this way until you complete the christie. If you hold the poles this way you are forced to angulate properly. This is a good exercise to use whenever you have trouble with body positioning.

If desired, use your poles in the uphill christie. The timing and positioning of the pole plant is important and must be practiced. The pole should be placed midway between your ski tip and boot as you sink down to unweight. Withdraw the pole as you come up. Stand on the flat and practice placing the right and left poles alternately. For safety, plant each pole with your palm turned up. In this way you will avoid accidentally running into the pole. Sink down and plant the right pole; rise up, remove the right pole; sink down and place the left pole; rise up, etc. Continue placing your poles alternately until you establish a steady rhythm and consistently plant the pole in the correct location. When this is easily done, practice the pole plants while moving down a gentle slope in the straight running position. After this can be done rhythmically, try an uphill christie with the pole plant. At the completion of your first down motion, lightly touch the pole to the snow on your turning side. When turning right, touch the right pole to the snow; when turning left, touch the left pole to the snow. To avoid confusion, remember that you always make your turn around your pole; it will always be on the inside of your turn as a pivot point around which your turn is made. Remove the pole as your body passes it. Use the pole only as a pivot, not as a crutch.

Remember to sink down and rise up to flatten your skis and to release the edges. It also unweights the tails so they can skid. Once the skis begin to skid, be sure to sink down again to control the direction of the skid. Don't force the tails around. Just kneel and wait. The correct traverse position is maintained throughout the maneuver—body weight placed on downhill ski.

Practice on a fairly well-packed slope. The slope should be wide enough to provide room for the traverse and be a bit steeper than the hill on which you learned the stem turn. Begin practicing christies from a shallow traverse, gradually increasing the angle of the traverse until you are nearly parallel to the fall line when you begin your christie. Master christies to both the left and right.

Now that you have mastered the uphill christie you have experienced the thrill of graceful, effortless skiing. You have reached a level of skill where you can ski in control on nearly any advanced novice slope. You may wish to advance from your status as a beginning intermediate skier. If so, you will not find parallel turns too far away; the uphill christie is the bridge to these long awaited turns.

Whatever your skill, whenever you ski, take time to appreciate the scenery and the camaraderie. It is all a part of the charm and enchantment of skiing.

TERMINOLOGY

American Ski Technique—Official sequence of instruction taught by the Professional Ski Instructors of America and its member schools.

Angulation—Sideways bending of the upper body toward the outside of a turn or away from the hill when traversing.

Balanced Stance—The most normal position possible for good, controlled skiing.

Basket—The ring attached near the tip of a ski pole which serves to keep the pole from sinking too deeply into the snow.

Boot Press—Device to hold and carry ski boots when not in use. Boots are clamped in tightly so the soles remain flat.

Camber—The slight upward arch or bow in the middle of the ski which supports the skier's weight and distributes it along the entire length of the ski.

Christie—Fundamental turn in intermediate and advanced skiing in which the skis are held parallel during the completion of the maneuver. Short for Christiania.

Comma Position—The curved or comma-like appearance of the body which results from angulation. The upper body is leaned away from the hill while the knees and hips press into the hill.

Counterrotation—Vigorous preparatory motion or wind-up in the initiation of a turn. The upper body turns in the opposite direction of the lower body. This movement of the upper body in opposition to movement of the lower body is usually performed by drawing back the outside, or uphill hip and shoulder.

Downhill Ski (Leg, Shoulder, etc.)—The ski (or leg or shoulder, etc.) which is closer to the bottom of the slope. As the skier skis down a slope in a series of S turns, each ski alternates between being the downhill and the uphill ski.

Down-unweighting—Means of momentarily reducing body weight on the skis. Accomplished by a sharp dropping or lowering of the body at the ankles, knees, hips and waist.

Edge Control—The adjustment of the angle between the skis' running surface and the snow.

Edges—The tempered steel strips affixed to the outer corners of the underside, or running surface, of each ski. They run the length of the ski on either side and provide lateral adhesion during turns and traverses on hardpacked or icy slopes.

Edging—Tilting the skis so one edge of each ski presses into the snow.

Fall Line—Fastest and most direct route from top to bottom of hill. The imaginary line of least resistance a freely rolling ball would take down the slope if affected only by gravity. The line is always established according to the skier's immediate location.

Forward Lean—Leaning the body directly forward from the ankles and flexing the knees so the weight of the body is carried on the balls of the feet. This causes the body weight to be distributed over the forward portion of the skis.

Grip—Handle on a ski pole made to fit the contour of the hand.

Groove—Indentation running down the middle of the bottom of a ski which aids in straight running, tracking and traversing.

Heel Thrust—Pushing down and out with the heels during a turn or traverse, causing the tails of the skis to be displaced.

Herringbone—A climbing method in which the skis are stepped up the hill in a V-position with the tails close together and tips apart. Each ski is stepped uphill alternately with pressure exerted against the inside edges. Leaves a herringbone tweed pattern in the snow.

Inside Edge—The edge of the ski nearest to the other ski.

Kick Turn—A method of reversing one's direction on skis by kicking one ski into the air, reversing it, and stepping the second ski around. Most often used when stationary.

Linked Turns—Series of consecutive turns in alternating directions in which the end of one turn is the beginning of another.

Mogul—Large mound of snow on a slope formed partly by the natural terrain underneath the snow, but caused mostly when a number of skiers turn in the same place and kick the snow into a pile. The skiers' turning action digs a trough and at the same time moves the loose snow onto the bump.

National Ski Patrol System (NSPS)—American organization of volunteers highly trained in mountain first aid, rescue skills and ski safety. The members patrol ski slopes and render assistance wherever necessary.

Outside Edge—The ski edge farthest from the other ski.

Outside Ski—The ski describing the outside arc of a turn. The ski which is weighted in order to turn in a new direction.

Parallel—Any maneuver, usually a turn, performed with the skis parallel. A style of skiing in which the skis point in the same direction throughout all maneuvers.

Pole Plant—Placing the tip of the inside ski pole into the snow prior to making a turn or a jump.

Professional Ski Instructors of America (PSIA)—Association of certified professional ski instructors, which formulated the American Ski Technique and establishes standards for organized ski instruction in the United States.

Release Binding—Device mounted on a ski which fastens it to the boot. Incorporates a release factor that separates the ski from the boot when a preset tension is exceeded due to excess stress or pressure.

Reverse Shoulder—Distinctive body position in which the upper body faces downhill or to the outside of a turn. The legs move in one direction while the upper body moves in the opposite direction to compensate for forces involved.

Safety Strap—Strap which attaches to boot and ski to prevent a released ski from hurtling down the slope.

Schuss—Skiing straight downhill without turning or checking speed.

Schussboomer—One who schusses, usually carelessly and out of control. Likely to end up in the first aid room.

Shaft—Main portion of the ski pole.

Shovel—Upturned portion at the very front of the ski.

Sideslip—Sideways slipping of the skis down the hill while they are held parallel and the tips are pointing across the hill.

Sidestepping—Method of climbing straight up a slope in which the skis are stepped uphill alternately while kept at right angles to the fall line.

Sitz Mark—The impression made in the snow by a fallen skier. Also known as a "bathtub."

Skating—Moving skis in a skating fashion to gain speed on a flat stretch or at the beginning of a run.

Slope—Generic term for ski terrain, generally applied to a specific part of hill.

Snowplow—A basic maneuver used in skiing to control speed or to stop.

Snowplow Turn—An elementary turn used to negotiate simple changes of direction. The snowplow position is held throughout the turn.

Stem Christie—Moderate and high speed skid turn started with a stem. Skis are brought parallel at the fall line or just before it.

Stem Turn—Slow speed turn in which the skis start together in a traverse. The tail of one ski is then moved away from the other ski into a V-position to initiate the turn. The skis are brought parallel again after the skier has crossed the fall line and is moving in his new traverse.

Stemming—Opening the tail of the uphill ski away from the downhill ski so the skis are in a V-position with the tips close together and the tails spread apart. This aids in initiating a turn.

Straight Running—Skiing straight downhill with the skis parallel.

Strap—Loop attached to the ski pole at the grip, which holds the pole on the wrist.

Tail—Portion of the ski behind the binding.

Terrain—Configuration of skiable surface of any mountain.

Tip—The portion of the ski in front of the mid-point or binding.

Total Motion—The concept that while skiing, the body and all its parts must be in continuous motion in order to maintain good balance. No single part of the body is moved without making compensating adjustments with the rest of the body.

Traverse—To ski straight across or diagonally down the hill with the skis parallel. The single most important position in skiing.

Unweighting—Momentary removal of body weight from the skis to permit the initiating of a maneuver or the releasing of the edges. It may be accomplished with either a quick up-motion or down-motion of the body.

Up-unweighting—A momentary removal of body weight from the skis accomplished by a quick upward extension of the body. This eliminates some friction under the skis, making it easier to turn them.

Vertical Drop—The height of a ski slope from top to bottom.

Weight Transfer—A movement of body weight toward one ski. Often referred to as weighting the ski. A source of turning power.

BIBLIOGRAPHY

Beattie, Bob. *My Ten Secrets of Skiing.* New York: The Viking Press, 1968.

Bourdon, Bob. *The New Way to Ski.* New York: Universal Publishing and Distributing Corp., 1962.

Editors. *Sports Illustrated Book of Skiing.* New York: J.B. Lippincott Co., 1957.

Editors of "Ski Magazine." *The Skier's Handbook.* New York: Harper and Row, 1965.

Eriksen, Stein. *Come Ski With Me.* New York: W.W. Norton and Co., 1966.

Estin, Peter. *Skiing the American Way.* New York: The John Day Co., 1964.

Jay, John. *Ski Down the Years.* New York: Universal Publishing Corp., 1966.

Joubert, Georges and Jean Vuarnet. *How to Ski the New French Way.* New York: The Dial Press, Inc., 1967.

Kramer, Franz. *Ski the New Way.* New York: Sterling Publishing Co., Inc., 1958.

Landers, Chris. *Learn to Ski.* New York: Rand McNally and Co., 1969.

McCulloch, Ernie. *Ski the Champion's Way.* New York: Harper and Row, 1967.

Polasek, Ollie. *Skiing.* New York: A.S. Barnes and Co., Inc., 1960.

Professional Ski Instructors of America. *The Official American Ski Technique.* New York: Cowles Book Company, Inc., 1964.

Rose, Jack and Mike Erickson, eds. *Old Crow Alpine Skier's Guide.* Largo, Florida: Snibbe Sports, Inc., 1969.

Shambroom, Rick and Betty Slater. *Skiing With Control.* London: Collier-Macmillan Ltd., 1965.

Siggins, Maggie. *Guide to Eastern Ski Resorts.* New York: McGraw-Hill, 1969.

Sullivan, George. *The Complete Book of Family Skiing.* New York: Coward-McCann, Inc., 1966.

SWIMMING

BEHAVIORAL OBJECTIVES

1. In a pool with a depth of at least five feet, the college student will be able to successfully demonstrate (meet *all* of the essential criteria as specified in the chapter) the following swimming fundamentals:
   a. Jelly-Fish Float.
   b. Supine Float.
   c. Prone Glide.
   d. Supine Glide.
   e. Bobbing.
   f. Sculling.
   g. Finning.
   h. Treading Water.
   i. Prone Crawl Stroke.
   j. Back Crawl Stroke.
   k. Sidestroke.
   l. Elementary Backstroke.
   m. Breaststroke.
2. The college student will be able to achieve a score of at least 75 per cent on a written examination concerned with the history, terminology, water safety and analysis of swimming fundamentals.

HISTORY OF SWIMMING

How or why man entered the waters has become lost in the maze of years before written history. There are indications of man being in the water and swimming prior to 1500 A.D. but these are very vague and known only by pictures drawn on cave walls.

Up until the Greek and Roman civilizations, it is believed that man swam only the *"doggie paddle"* or human stroke. By 880 B.C., the overhand stroke was being practiced. Ruins of Pompeii and Greek coins dated 193 A.D. definitely prove that the overhand stroke was known by the Ancient Romans.

It wasn't until 1538 that the first written word describing a stroke was put into print by Nicolaus Wynman, a German Professor. Around 1697, a Frenchman by the name of Thevenot, wrote a book entitled *The Art of Swimming.* This book describes the first efforts of man doing the breaststroke.

John Trudgen, in 1873, introduced the modern trudgen stroke, which is the forerunner to the development of the crawl stroke. Since then, swimming has become one of the leading recreational activities in America due to its use in survival measures, physical development, therapeutic purposes, as well as for recreational purposes.

NATURE OF SWIMMING

Man is not physiologically built for the water. He is handicapped primarily because he is an upright creature. Over the years, however, man has become quite proficient in the art of swimming.

The beginning swimmer, regardless of his chronological age, has to prepare himself psychologically before entering the water. The swimmer must remember that he is entering a new environment in which there will more than likely be a temperature change on his body. In addition, when in chest-deep water, there will be added pressure on the chest cavity which will require an adjustment in his breathing pattern. Hundreds of thousands of people have mastered the skills of swimming. The beginning swimmer must begin his new endeavor with a positive approach; with the full knowledge that he too can learn to swim.

EQUIPMENT

The swimmer should remember that heavy material and bulky suits will inhibit his progress. It is recommended that the swimmer wear a *tank suit.*

SKILLS TO BE DEVELOPED

Jelly-fish Float

The jelly-fish float is started from a standing position in chest-deep water. The body bends forward and the hands are placed on the thighs. A deep inhalation is taken and the body bends further forward so the face is submerged. The hands then slide down along the outside of the legs to the ankles. This movement is done slowly in a relaxed manner. The feet will leave the bottom. The body will be floating in a suspended balanced position with a portion of the back showing above the surface of the water. (See Figure 9-1a)

To regain a standing position the head and upper body are raised toward the surface, and the feet are placed on the bottom.

Supine Float

Start by standing in chest-deep water or holding on to the side of the pool. The shoulders are submerged just below the surface. A deep inhalation is taken as the head slowly moves back until the ears are submerged and the chin is pointing upward. The arms are extended and move sideward through the water to a position above the shoulders. As the body drifts backward the feet should leave the bottom. (See Figure 9-1b)

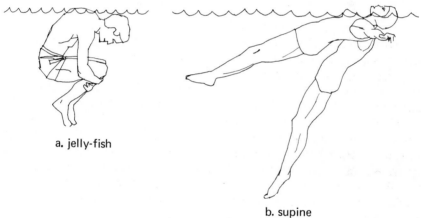

a. jelly-fish

b. supine

Figure 9-1. Floating.

To regain a standing position the hips are dropped, the chin is brought forward, and the arms are swept forward. This action will bring the feet under the body so an upright position can be attained.

Bobbing

This is a skill of alternating the projection of the body below and above the surface of the water by using the arms and legs. Inhalation occurs when the head is above the surface, and exhalation occurs beneath the surface. Bobbing can first be practiced in chest-deep water and later in deeper depths.

Starting with the head above the water, inhale, and sweep the arms upward—this will enable the head to submerge, and exhalation takes place. The feet push off the bottom and the arms press the water downward—this will bring the head above the surface again for inhalation. Exhalation must be forceful in order to be ready to inhale quickly as the head is above the surface for a very short period of time.

Treading

This is a method of maintaining the head above water, with the body in a vertical position, using minimum effort. This skill can first be practiced by holding on to the side of the pool with one hand.

The arms are just below the shoulder level. The hands move in wide circles as the palms press downward. A slow, wide flutter, breaststroke, or scissors kick can be used (refer to strokes).

Finning

This is a method of propelling the body head first in a supine position by using the arms as a means of propulsion. It involves a series of up and backward movements of the forearms and hands.

Start in a back glide with the arms extended at the sides of the body. The hands move slowly upward along the sides of the body to the upper hip. The wrists then hyperextend so the palms are facing backward. The palms forcefully push the water toward the feet as the elbows extend and the arms return to the starting position.

Sculling

This skill is for keeping the body afloat, or for propulsion. The hands perform an outward and then inward motion through the water while applying force opposite the desired direction of progress. To scull forward, start in a supine glide with the arms relaxed in a position close to the sides of the body. While performing the outward and inward movements, the wrists lead and the fingertips are angled slightly upward toward the surface. The hands describe a pattern similar to the infinity sign as the palms continuously apply force in the direction of the feet. The elbows are slightly flexed throughout the skill.

Basic Principles

1. One should always streamline himself in the water, always keep the body as close to the surface of the water as possible.
2. For every action there is an equal and opposite reaction. This means that force should be applied in the direction *opposite* to the desired movement through the water—pull back to go forward.
3. A body in motion tends to stay in motion while a body at rest tends to stay at rest. Implication to swimming is that more energy is needed to start a stroke and less energy will be needed to sustain the stroke after the initial exertion is started.

In learning the strokes, the following progression will be analyzed:
Body Position.
Leg Action.
Arm Action.
Breath Control.
Coordination.

Prone Crawl

The prone crawl is the fastest and most efficient stroke. The prone position enables the arms to drive the water almost directly backwards. Rotation of the head for breathing makes the crawl unique among the other basic strokes.

Body Position. (Prone Glide) Push off the side of the pool with your feet. Extend body in a *prone* (on stomach) position. The body should be streamlined with the arms extended overhead and the legs together and straight. Execute a prone glide with your head well above the surface of the water. Try again with your face submerged and notice how your legs stay up for a longer period of time. Experiment with the prone glide changing the water level on your head to see which position is best for you—it should be somewhere between eyebrows and hairline.

Leg Action (Flutter Kick) On your side, extend bottom arm and support it with a kick board—perform a walking *(flutter)* motion with legs through the water; this movement is initiated from the hips. Try the same skill on your other side, then in a prone position.

In alternating the up and down action of the legs, the knee and ankle remain relaxed. When effecting the *down-beat*, the hip and knees are flexed. On completing the *up-beat* the leg is straight with a relaxed ankle. The heel should just break the surface of the water.

Due to the anatomical structure of the ankle and the foot, the water pressure, and the desired relaxation, a toeing-in effect results. The toeing-in should not be forced by the swimmer since to do so would negate the necessary and desired relaxed ankle and foot.

The kick mainly serves to balance and stabilize the effects of the swinging motion of the arms and the rolling of the body. Therefore, the swimmer should not consciously force the alternating up and down beats of the legs in attempting forward progress, but should relax the legs and let them automatically react from the movements of the arms and torso.

Arm Action. (Pull and Recover) The arms exert a constant force to drive water toward the feet in a continuous, alternating action. The pattern of the arm movements can be broken down to a *propulsive phase* and a *recovery phase.*

Start with the arm extended in front of the shoulder and pull the water toward the feet. The position of the arm should be slightly flexed at the elbow, wrist extended, and fingers relaxed. When the arm is below the shoulder it pushes back—a direction opposite that of the intended movement. The line of force should be parallel to the midline of the body. The basic description of the arms' propulsive phase is a *pull-push* action. On completing this phase the arm ends in an extended position on the lateral part of the body.

The arm recovers up and over the water with the elbow high and leading the way. The lift of the arm is initiated at the shoulder joint. The arm is extended just prior to being placed in the water (fingertips first) in line with the shoulder. A slight body roll will ease the recovery action. One stroke is the completion of both arms through one recovery phase and one propulsive phase.

Breath Control. Rhythmic breathing can be practiced in shallow water or at the side of the pool. Lean forward so the upper part of the body assumes a prone position. Place one side of the face in the water so that the ear is submerged. Inhale quickly through the mouth. Rotate head to a face down position and exhale. Then rotate head to the side again for inhalation. This cycle is repeated in a continuous, rhythmic sequence, Practice rhythmic breathing to one side and then the other to determine your natural breathing side.

While swimming, the inhalation phase is short and the exhalation longer. In performing the prone crawl, inhalation takes place as the head is rotated to one side just enough to bring the mouth to the surface. Even though breathing may occur on either side the swimmer usually develops a preference or "breathing side." Inhalation should occur as the arm on the breathing side is starting the last half of the propulsive phase and the opposite arm has just entered the water and is starting to pull. Due to the positioning of the head and forward movement of the swimmer through the water, an air pocket is created by the flow of water about the head. This enables the swimmer to inhale below the surface level, and therefore minimize head rotation.

Exhalation occurs immediately through the nose and mouth with a steady flow of air as the head rotates to a face down position. Then rotation of the head smoothly reverses to turn the face to the breathing side and ready for inhalation. A breathing cycle is the pattern of inhalation and exhalation per one stroke.

Coordination. From a prone glide, start the arm pull on your breathing side. Rotate head and inhale as arm is completing the power phase. The arm on the non-breathing side starts to pull, the head is rotated face downward, exhalation starts, and the breathing side arm recovers. The non-breathing side arm recovers as the breathing side arm starts to pull. (See Figure 9-2)

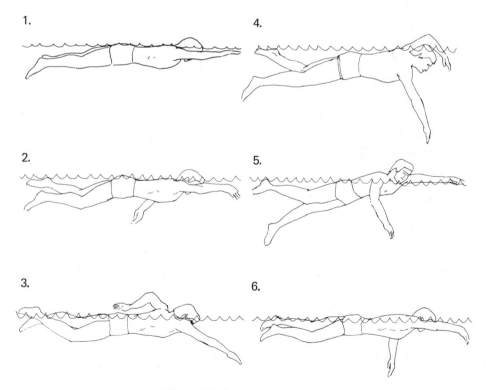

Figure 9-2. Prone Crawl Stroke.

Once you feel comfortable coordinating the arms with breathing, add the leg action. A *6-beat kick* is most common, but a 4-beat or 2-beat is sometimes preferred by the swimmer.

There is no glide phase in the prone crawl stroke. The swimmer is continuously moving in an even rhythm similar to Waltz music.

Back Crawl Stroke

The back crawl is one of the four competitive strokes. As in the prone (front) crawl, the action is continuous; there is an alternating *pull* and *recovery* armstroke and a constant *flutter kick*. The supine body position allows for free breathing.

Body Position. (Supine glide) The body should be in a back-glide horizontal position. The head is in line with the spine and submerged to the level of the ears. The legs are fully extended and together. The arms are extended at the sides of the body.

Leg Movement. (Flutter kick) As in the front crawl, the legs alternate in an up and down action. This action is initiated at the hip, with sequential joint action occurring at the knee and ankle. On the *up* beat the knee is flexed and the ankle is passively extended. The upper surface of the lower leg and the foot apply maximum force backward as the knee extends forcefully. On completing the up beat, the foot is brought to the surface with the toes just breaking the surface.

The downward leg action starts at the hip joint with the knee and ankle remaining relaxed and slightly flexed. At the end of the down beat the knee and ankle joints extend to apply force against the water with the back surface of the leg and sole.

Arm Movement. (Windmill) The arms rotate backward in an alternating propulsive and recovery phase. This action is continuous so a constant force is applied to drive water toward the feet.

With the arm extended at the side, the recovery phase begins by lifting the arm from the water with the wrist and elbow slightly flexed. The arm is swung upward in a vertical plane. The wrist and elbow extend when the arm passes over the shoulder. With the little finger leading, the hand enters the water in line with the shoulder. The swimmer then rolls slightly on the long axis of the body to lower the hand (12" deep) in position for the propulsive phase.

The palm and inner surface of the arm are directed toward the feet in an outward and backward sweeping movement. When the arm reaches shoulder level the elbow is flexed and the hand is rotated to push downward to full extension at the side. This final downward action will lift the shoulder nearer the surface to aid in a smooth recovery.

Breath Control. Inhale through the mouth and exhale through the nose and mouth. One breath cycle should be executed for each complete arm cycle.

Coordination. (For a 6-beat stroke) As one arm executes the propulsive phase the other arm executes the recovery phase, each leg performs three kicks in opposition, and inhalation occurs.

The opposite arm executes the propulsive action as the other arm executes the recovery phase, each leg executes three kicks in opposition, and exhalation occurs.

As one arm is recovering the opposite leg is kicking upward. (See Figure 9-3)

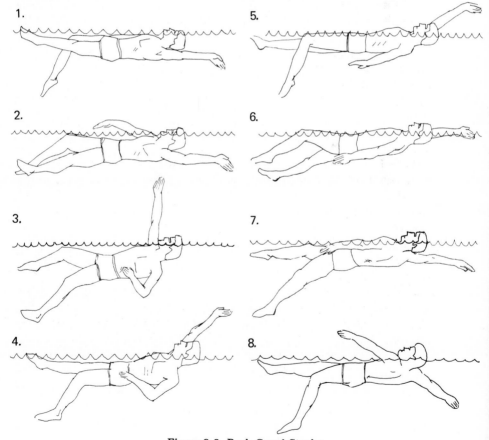

Figure 9-3. Back Crawl Stroke.

Sidestroke

Unlike the prone crawl the sidestroke is a *resting* stroke. It has an extended glide phase which enables the swimmer to rest in between strokes. The basic leg action is used in lifesaving carries, underwater swimming, and for survival techniques.

Body Position. The body is extended in a horizontal position on its side with the lower arm overhead in line with the body. The top arm is extended along the side with the palm of the hand in contact with the thigh. The head is aligned with the body and cradled against the water so the lower side of the face is slightly below the surface of the water. Focus should be toward the feet.

Leg Action. (Scissor Kick) In a bracket position—lie on one side, top hand on pool edge, bottom hand underwater with fingers downward press against side of pool with palm—extend legs in a horizontal position perpendicular to the side of the pool.

The recovery phase is initiated by a slow flexion and separation of the legs. The top leg is forward and flexed at the hip, knee, and ankle. The bottom leg is backward, hyperextended a the hip, flexed knee, and extended ankle. At the completion of the recovery phase the legs are in a wide stride or hurdle position.

Without stopping the propulsive phase follows. The feet, sole of forward foot and instep of back foot, press backward and finally inward to the centerline. As the feet come together the knees are extended and the water is squeezed from in between the legs. Both legs execute the propulsive action simultaneously, with the legs ending together and fully extended for the glide phase.

The scissors kick can easily be practiced with a kick board in the hand of the bottom arm.

Arm Action. The bottom arm starts its propulsive action by flexing the elbow so that the palm and inside of the arm presses backward toward the feet. When the arm and hand have pressed back past the shoulder, the elbow stays close to the body, and the hand continues to press back.

For the recovery phase, the elbow flexes to its maximum and is drawn close to the body while the forearm rotates outward and parallel to the trunk. The back of the hand is positioned close to the lower shoulder. The fingertips then lead the arm in extension as it returns to the overhead starting position. The entire arm action is under the surface.

The top arm is recovered from its extended position at the thigh by sliding the hand, with the thumb leading, to a position approximately in front of the shoulder. Keep the arm close to the body throughout the recovery phase to eliminate negative resistance.

Rotate the forearm outward so the palm is toward the feet. In executing the propulsive action the palm and the inside of the forearm push toward the feet as the elbow extends. The arm is fully extended and the palm is on the thigh at the completion of the propulsive phase: The arm is held in this position for the glide.

Breath Control. Inhale through the mouth during the recovery phase of the top arm and the legs.

Exhale through the nose and mouth as the top arm and the legs are effecting their propulsive actions. Exhalation occurs throughout the glide also.

Coordination. The recovery and propulsive phases of the top arm and legs coincide. The extended lower arm starts its propulsive action and inhalation starts. The top arm and legs recover. As the bottom arm completes recovery into the extended position, the top arm pushes back and the legs kick. Exhale! Both arms and legs hold the extended glide position. (See Figure 9-4)

Figure 9-4. Sidestroke.

Breaststroke

The breaststroke is not only a resting stroke, but is also one of the four strokes used in competition. With slight variations, it is also used in lifesaving techniques.

Body Position. The body is in a prone position. Arms are extended in front of the head with the palms down. The legs are together and extended with the hips and feet below the surface. The body is streamlined in a near-horizontal position.

Leg Action. (Whip Kick) The recovery starts by a slow, easy flexion of the knees to draw the heels toward the trunk just below the surface of the water. There is minimal hip flexion. As the heels reach a point over the knees, the ankles flex and pronate, and the toes point to the sides. Simultaneously, the knees will spread slightly—8 to 12 inches—but not as wide as the distance between the feet.

The propulsive phase of the legs is effected by bringing the feet outward and backward through an arc while the hips, knees, and ankles are extended. In this action, the soles of the feet and inner surface of the lower legs forcefully press backward against the water causing the forward propulsion of the body. The kick finishes with the legs extended for the glide position.

This kick can be practiced in a vertical position at the side of the pool, in a bracket position, and finally with a kick board.

Arm Action. The propulsive phase is initiated by the hands separating and moving diagonally outward and downward. The elbows begin to bend slightly and are kept high. The palms and inside of the arms pull back toward the feet, but never go beyond the elbows. The elbows should neither be higher than the shoulders, nor go beyond the shoulders.

During the last part of this action the arms recover against the chest and the hands are brought close together, palms downward, in front of the chest. The hands lead the arms into the overhead extended position.

By holding a kick board between the legs a swimmer can practice the arm movements in a prone position through the water.

Breath Control. Inhale through the mouth at the completion of the propulsive phase of the arms: This is done by hyperextending the neck so that the head lifts high enough for just the mouth to clear the surface.

Exhalation occurs after the face is lowered to the water and throughout the rest of the stroke.

Coordination. Pull, breath, kick, glide is the basic sequence for effecting the stroke. The arms pull; inhalation occurs. As the arms complete the propulsive phase and begin recovery, the legs recover, and exhalation starts. The legs kick while the arms extend to complete the recovery (continue to exhale). Glide in a prone, extended position, and finish exhaling. (See Figure 9-5)

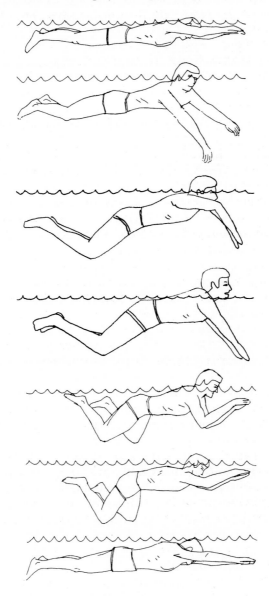

Figure 9-5. Breaststroke.

Elementary Backstroke

The elementary backstroke is basically a resting stroke. The relaxed, paired movement of the arms and legs is easy to coordinate.

Body Position. The body is extended in a *supine* (on back) position. The arms at the sides, and the head is submerged to about ear level. The actions of the arms and legs are performed beneath the surface of the water.

Leg Action (Whip Kick) The legs are together and extended. From this position they start the recovery phase. The knees and ankles flex so that the heels drop down and back. The thighs remain in line with the body, below and parallel to the surface of the water. As the heels approach the hips, and are at a point directly below the knees, the feet rotate so the toes point to the sides. The ankles are still flexed and the feet pronated in order to place the soles in the direction in which the force is to be applied. Simultaneously, the knees spread slightly and the feet separate to their maximum (the feet are a greater distance apart than the knees). All recovery movements should be slow and smooth to minimize resistance.

The propulsive action takes place as the lower part of the legs and feet thrust backward and upward against the water forming an arc. The knees maintain a partially flexed position until the feet come together at the end of the kick. Near the end of the kick the ankles forcefully extend from their flexed position to increase propulsion.

This kick can be practiced in a supine bracket position—head rests on edge of pool, hands close to ears, palms down, hold onto edge of pool, extend legs to a position perpendicular to the side of the pool. The swimmer can then try a kick board and hold it in the same manner as the bracket position, but move through the water.

Arm Action. Starting with a glide with the arms extended at the sides, the recovery phase occurs first. The elbows are flexed as the hands are slowly drawn up the sides of the torso toward the shoulders. To minimize resistance the hands and elbows should be kept as close to the body as possible during this movement. When the hands reach a position just below the shoulders, the forearms rotate to place the fingers facing outward to the sides. With the fingers leading and the palms facing backward, the arms are extended to a point slightly above shoulder level.

The propulsive action takes place when the palms and inner surface of the arms push the water forcefully toward the feet. At the completion of this broad, sweeping action the arms are at their extended position at the sides with the hands on the thighs.

Breath Control. Inhale through the mouth as the arms and legs are recovering.

Exhale through the nose and mouth during the propulsive phase of the stroke.

Coordination. With the legs extended and the arms at the sides, the arms start the stroke with the recovery action; inhale.

As the hands reach the waist, the legs start to recover; inhale.

The arms and legs complete their recovery phases and simultaneously execute the propulsive action; exhale.

The glide takes place in the extended position; exhale. (See Figure 9-6)

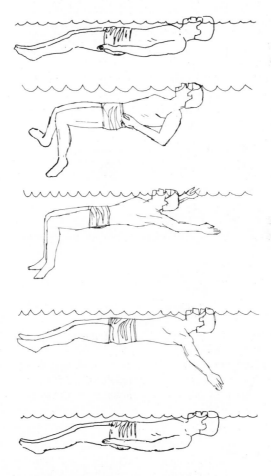

Figure 9-6. Elementary Backstroke.

TERMINOLOGY

Bobbing—The alternate projection of the body, using the arms and legs, below the surface (exhalation) and above the surface (inhalation).

Finning—A method of propelling the body head first in a supine position by using the arms as a means of propulsion. It involves a series of up and backward movements of the forearms and hands.

Flexion—The bending of a joint (e.g., wrist, knee, ankle.).

Floating—It is the ability to rest on the surface or be suspended in the water.

Prone Glide—The body is in a streamlined, facedown, near-horizontal position. The arms are extended beyond the head, and the legs extended back.

Propulsive Phase—The action of a stroke which contributes to the intended progress of the swimmer.

Recovery Phase—The action of a stroke which positions the body or parts of the body to a position that enables propulsion to begin.

Sculling—A method of keeping the body afloat or of propulsion by using the arms. For propulsion the hands perform an outward and then inward motion while applying force opposite the desired direction of progress through the water.

Supine Glide—A near-horizontal position on the back. The legs are extended and together. The arms are extended overhead.

Treading—A method of maintaining the head above water, with the body in a vertical position, using minimum effort.

BIBLIOGRAPHY

American Red Cross, *Swimming and Water Safety*, Washington, D.C.: American National Red Cross, 1968.

Broer, Marion R., *Efficiency of Human Movement*, Second Edition. Philadelphia and London: W.B. Saunders Company, 1966.

Councilman, James E., *The Science of Swimming*, Englewood Cliffs, N.J.: Prentice Hall, Inc., 1968.

Gabrielson, M. Alexander, Spears, Betty and Gabrielson, B.W., *Aquatics Handbook*, Englewood Cliffs, N.J.: Prentice Hall, Inc., 1968.

Gambril Donald J., *Swimming*, ed. J. Tullman Hall. California: Goodyear Publishing Company, 1969.

Harris, Marjorie M., *Basic Swimming Analyzed*, Boston: Allyn and Bacon, Inc., 1969.

Scott, M. Gladys, *Analysis of Human Motion*, Second Edition. New York: Appleton-Century-Crofts, Division of Meredith Publishing Company, 1963.

Vickers, Betty J. and Vincent, William J., *Swimming*, Dubuque, Iowa: Wm. C. Brown Company, 1966.

TENNIS

BEHAVIORAL OBJECTIVES

1. Given a tennis racket, under simulated game conditions, the college student will be able to successfully demonstrate (meet *all* the essential criteria as specified in the chapter) the following tennis fundamentals:
   a. Eastern Grip.
   b. Backhand Grip.
   c. Western Grip.
   d. Ready Position.
   e. Forehand Ground Stroke.
   f. Backhand Ground Stroke.
   g. Flat Service.
   h. Slice Service.
   i. Volley.
2. The college student will be able to achieve a score of at least 75 per cent on a written examination concerned with the history, rules, terminology, strategy and analysis of tennis fundamentals.

HISTORY OF TENNIS

The present game of tennis has little resemblance to the French game, *Jue de Paume*, which was played as early as 1300 A.D. Originally, the game was played with the hands, but soon evolved into a racket sport. The size of the court dimensions and rules were in no way similar to our modern day game. The French term, "Tenez," which literally means *Take it! Play*, probably accounts for the name as we know it today. During the sixteenth and seventeenth century, the game enjoyed a wide scope of popularity in France and England. The game declined in popularity in the eighteenth century and only the wealthy played the game by the nineteenth century.

Major Walter Clapton Wingfield is credited with inventing and introducing tennis in England in 1873. He combined elements of *rackets*, *badminton*, and *court tennis* to obtain a game called *Sphairistike* which is the forerunner of today's game. The game of tennis was introduced to the United States by Miss Mary Weing Outerbridge in the spring of 1874.

Tournament play began to emerge after the United States Lawn Tennis Association was founded in 1881. In 1900, the Davis Cup tournament began which symbolizes world amateur team championship, competition, teams from all over the world. In 1923, the Wightman tournament began with matches between women's teams of the United States and England. Other famous matches which give tennis that international flair is the Wimbledon in England and the United States National Tournament at Forest Hills.

Throughout the past century the number of participants in the game has increased at a staggering pace. The game is no longer a game of the classes, but a game of the masses. With the introduction of the open tennis tournament, where amateurs and professionals may compete together, tennis has taken on a new look both for player and spectator.

NATURE OF TENNIS

Rules and scoring in tennis are standardized and do not change from country to country, on private or public courts, and apply both indoors and outdoors. The game is played on a court 78' long and 36' wide, divided by a tautly strung net 3'6" high at the posts, but only 3' high in the center. Singles is played by two players on a smaller court 27' wide. Doubles is played by four players, two on each team, on a 36' wide court. Each player uses a racket made of wood, metal, or plastic components in various combinations and strung with nylon or gut in order to stroke a rubber felt covered ball back and forth across the net.

The game begins when one player standing behind the baseline to the right of the center mark tosses the ball and serves it to his opponent. The serve must go over the net and land in the proper service area. If the serve is unsuccessful the server has another opportunity to serve. If the second serve is not successful, the server *faults* and the receiver wins a point. The next point is started from the left of the center mark and the serve is directed to the left service court. Successive services establish the right-left-right pattern until the game is won or lost.

If the serve is good, the receiver must return the ball into the opponent's court. The rally continues until one player hits the ball into the net or outside his opponent's court boundaries, or the ball bounces twice in his court. If a player's body, clothing or racket touch the net while the ball is in play, or if he reaches over the net to play a ball (unless the ball has bounced back over the net due to spin or to the wind) it is also a fault.

The server's ball must bounce once into the proper service court but after the serve a player may elect to either *ground stroke* the ball by hitting it on one bounce or *volley* the ball by hitting it before it bounces. At the end of the first game the server becomes the receiver and the receiver the server. Players change sides of court after each odd game (1, 3, 5). A player must win at least four points to win a game and have a two-point margin in the point total. Scoring in tennis is *15* for the first point, *30* for the second point, *40* for the third point and *game* for the fourth point. If the game is tied 40-40, or 3 points apiece it is called *deuce* and one player must win two consecutive points to win the game. A *set* in tennis is composed of at least six games and in order to win a set, a player must win a minimum of six games and have a two game lead over his opponent to conclude the set. A *match* is composed of three sets; to win a match a player must win two sets.

EQUIPMENT

The use of proper equipment by no means insures the tennis player success in his play, but it cannot hinder his performance. If you are endeavoring to purchase equipment and get involved in the game it is necessary to understand the strengths and weaknesses of available equipment.

Tennis Balls

Tennis balls are constructed from wool, felt, natural, synthetic or cold rubber. The hollow inside of the ball is inflated with compressed air or gas. In order to maintain the air pressure within the ball, balls are packaged in pressurized cans. Quality balls usually come in pressurized cans. Balls which have all their fuzz worn off them are termed "skinned," and frequently force the novice player who uses them into bad stroke habits. At one time all tennis balls were white. Now they may be obtained in an assortment of colors. Yellow-colored balls have been used for night play because of their added visibility. Heavy duty balls are covered with more felt or fuzz and, because of their construction, last longer. In purchasing tennis balls, the label "approved by the USLTA" is an indicator that the balls meet the proper specifications and are suited for play.

Tennis Racket

A beginner should secure the assistance of a knowledgeable tennis player when selecting his first racket. It is not necessary to purchase the most expensive racket while learning to play. A medium-priced racket is quite adequate while learning the fundamentals of the game. There is no official rule or design to dictate the size or shape of the tennis racket. It is interesting to note that with no official requirements, tennis rackets are for the most part uniform in dimensions (27″ long and 9″ wide across the face). Rackets are strung with gut or nylon. Gut is used by better players because of its high degree of resiliency. Nylon, either braided or perfected, gives good play, is economical and an excellent choice for the average player. Rackets come in various weights and grip sizes. For best results, a racket should fit comfortably in the hand and be of a weight that is easily handled. A press which prevents the frame from warping in damp weather and a canvas type cover for the face of the racket are the added extras that insure long wear and performance from the racket you purchase. (See Figure 10-1)

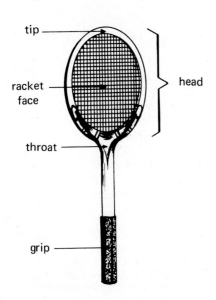

Figure 10-1. Tennis Racket.

Dress

The costume of the tennis player is white. This color is preferred to others because it reflects heat better; therefore it is the best to wear on a hot court. White is also less distracting to your opponent; thus it is worn as a courtesy to your opponent. Generally men wear t-shirts or knit shirts with collars and some type of white shorts. Women wear a feminine version of the knit shirt and shorts or a tennis dress. Finally, to round out your tennis attire, rubber soled tennis shoes, white fitting socks and a jacket or sweater are needed.

The Court

The dimensions of the playing court are standardized for singles and doubles. The playing surfaces are of many types: clay, cement, asphalt, grass, astroturf, and cork. The surface in many instances will affect the bounce and velocity of the ball.

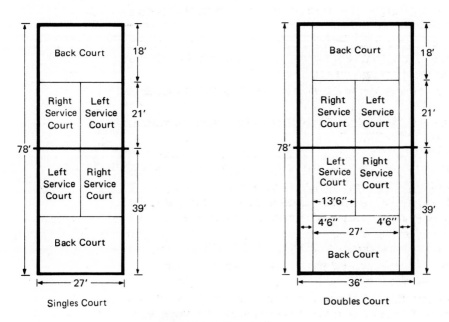

Figure 10-2. Tennis Court.

SKILLS TO BE DEVELOPED

This section will provide the beginning tennis player with fundamental skills which should be developed to enhance the level of skill of the tennis player. The beginner should keep in mind that tennis, as in other sport skills, has a "degree of flexibility." This degree of flexibility exists in all phases of the tennis game—from the grip of the racket, to the amount of backswing, to the proper point of impact on the ball. The beginner should start with the directions and skills presented. If these do not produce the results desired, the player may then begin to move into the "flexibility range." This is that range where a player may change some aspect of his game and still stay within the boundaries of proper skill techniques and in so doing, still play good tennis. The directions presented are for right handed players. Left handed players will need to reverse the directions.

Grip

There are three types of grips: *eastern, western,* and *continental.*

The Eastern Grip. This is the most widely used tennis grip because of its versatility to all phases of the tennis stroke. The Eastern forehand grip is often termed the "shake hands grip." Position the racket on its edge, racket face perpendicular to the ground. The racket handle is grasped as if you were shaking hands with the racket. The hand is placed so the heel is against the leather butt at the end of the handle. Spread the fingers, making certain the index finger is apart from the middle finger and is bent to form a trigger finger. The thumb and index finger should make a "V" just to the left of the center in the middle of the racket handle. (See Figure 10-3) The grip is firm enough for control, but not too tight or rigid. The backhand grip is obtained by moving the hand a quarter turn counterclockwise from the Eastern grip position, so the "V" between the thumb and forefinger is on the top left bevel or ridge of the grip and the thumb is diagonally across the back of the grip. The thumb may also be placed directly or in a parallel position along side the racket between the bevels. This technique will offer the beginner more support on executing the backhand. Remember, relax the grip between shots to avoid tiring the hand and arm. (See Figure 10-3)

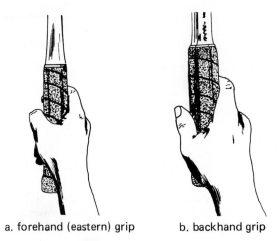

a. forehand (eastern) grip   b. backhand grip

Figure 10-3. The Grip.

The Continental Grip. To assume the continental grip, employ the same grip technique as that in the eastern backhand. It is not a desirable grip because of the strain on the forehand muscles and it is very difficult to stroke high bouncing balls.

The Western Grip. To perform the western grip, lay the racket flat on the court and simply pick it up. It is not used by many players because it is difficult to stroke low shots and volleys.

The Ready Position

The position which the tennis player assumes while waiting to return serve or to return a ball either forehand or backhand during play is called the *ready position.* It is the position which the player may easily move forward or back, left or right as efficiently and quickly as possible. This position is taken approximately three feet behind the baseline in the center when returning most baseline shots. When receiving service you will position yourself according to the type of serve your opponent may have, keeping in mind the same basic ready position. (See Figure 10-4)

Follow these steps:

1. Racket held firmly and directly in front of you.
2. Forehand grip on racket, left hand on throat of racket.
3. Body facing net, feet evenly spread, knees flexed, weight evenly distributed.

Figure 10-4. Ready Position.

Forehand Ground Stroke

The forehand ground stroke is the fundamental stroke and will serve as the keystone stroke in your entire game. Without a good, well-executed forehand your tennis game has little chance of improving.

There are five basic sequences in executing the ground strokes: (a) pivot, (b) backswing, (c) forward swing, (d) contacting the ball, and (e) follow through.

Pivot. As the ball approaches the player in the ready position, the player has two pivots he may use depending on his ability and preferences: (a) pivot on the left foot and place the right foot behind the body so that you are facing the side line of the court; your right foot assumes a position which is approximately two feet behind the left foot and positioned where a straight line (with some degree of variance) will extend from both feet; (b) pivot on the right foot and place the left foot out in front of the right foot in such a position where a straight line will extend from left foot to the right foot.

Backswing. The backswing begins its initial movement during the pivot phase; the player is now facing the sideline and body weight shifts gradually to the rear foot. At the same time, the racket moves back through the player's hip region. As the racket moves through this area, the player must make sure he keeps the face of the racket up and does not let it drop below the hip region. The backswing continues until it reaches the six o'clock position. If the player were standing at a ready position he would be facing 12 o'clock or facing straight ahead. When the backswing begins, he moves the racket back and through the hip region of 3 o'clock and continues to the six o'clock position where the backswing stops. This movement is made from the shoulders with a slightly bent elbow and a small degree of roll by the forehand. The position of the racket is perpendicular to the ground.

Forward Swing. The player begins his forward swing from the six o'clock position by moving the racket forward in a straight line past three o'clock and at the same time his weight is being transferred from his rear foot to the front foot. The movement of the front foot is a slight step or slide forward.

Contacting the Ball. The racket is now in an area past the three o'clock position and moving forward to make contact with the ball. The racket position is parallel to the ground with the face up and flat. Contact with the ball should occur slightly in front of the forward foot. At the instant of contact the arm is fully extended with the wrist and grip right to prevent the racket from moving in the player's hand. The ball should be hit waist high when possible. If the ball is below waist height, bend the knees, take the racket down to waist high and stroke the ball. If it bounces above waist high move back and position yourself to play the ball at proper height.

Follow Through. As the racket contacts the ball the racket continues the forward swing "through the ball" in the direction of the intended target. Finish the stroke with the racket pointing between 10 and 12 o'clock if you were standing in the middle of a clock when you begin your stroke. This motion should give you the feeling of hitting the ball out. The rear foot stays in contact with the court and acts as an anchor to insure proper weight transfer. Pose and hold this position for a fraction of a second before returning to the ready position and your next shot. (See Figure 10-5)

Figure 10-5. Forehand Ground Stroke.

Backhand Ground Stroke

Grip. The backhand grip differs from the forehand in that the hand is shifted to the left a quarter of a turn so that the heel of the hand rests on top of the handle. This position is necessary in order to hit the ball with a flat face and allow for more control over the stroke. The change to the backhand grip is made during the pivot and backswing sequence of the stroke. If the changing of the grip presents a problem for the beginner it is suggested that the forehand grip be employed until all the other aspects of the backhand can be performed with proficiency. The forehand grip will open the face slightly, thus reducing the control of the backhand ground stroke.

Pivot. As the ball approaches, the player has two pivot options which may be used depending on his preference and the position of the ball. A pivot can be made on the right foot, placing the left foot behind the body. This maneuver will find the player facing the sideline. The left foot assumes a position approximately two feet behind the right foot with a straight line extending from the right foot to the left foot. A slight degree of variance may occur in this line depending on the position of the ball. Another method is to pivot on the left foot and place the right foot out in front of the left foot in such a position where once again a straight line extends from the right foot to the left foot with some degree of variance occurring depending on the position of the ball.

Backswing. The backswing is initiated when the player begins his pivot motion. The player is now facing the sideline and the body weight shifts gradually to the rear foot. At the same time the racket is moving back through the player's hip region. Make sure the racket face does not drop below the hips and the left hand is still positioned on the throat of the racket. Keep the left hand positioned on the throat of the racket until the racket reaches the six o'clock position. The positioning of the left hand in the backswing is an important phase of the backswing. It will insure more control during the stroke and place the racket in the proper position so the player will be able to execute the proper forward motion.

Forward Swing. The player begins his forward swing from the six o'clock position and the racket is positioned in an area between the hip and shoulder region. On the forward swing the left hand is released from the throat of the racket. As the racket begins its forward swing, the weight transfer occurs in a gradual motion from the left (back) to the right foot. As the racket is swung forward there is movement from the shoulders with the elbow slightly bent and farther away from the body than the forehand stroke. The shoulders are swung well around to the left for increased power and feet are approximately parallel and spread comfortably apart, toes toward the net.

Contacting the Ball. Contact with the ball is made slightly in front of the forward foot, with a flat or slightly open-faced racket. The arm is fully extended at contact and the wrist and grip of the racket is firm.

Follow Through. As in the forehand, a good follow through is necessary to impart power and direction to the ball. Do not stop the forward swing the instant you make contact. As the ball contacts the racket, the head continues through the ball in the direction of the target area. At the finish the hand is shoulder level or slightly higher and the racket is pointing to one or two o'clock. The left arm acts as a counter balance, remaining below the racket arm. The same applies to the left foot. It remains in contact with the court until the stroke is completed. The weight is on the forward foot and the knee is bent slightly, not stiff or locked. The body turn is complete as the body faces the net returning to the ready position. (See Figure 10-6)

The Serve

The service places the ball into play. It is the only time during tennis play when the player requires the skill and coordination of both hands. It is possibly the most essential skill to be learned and mastered. It is recommended that the beginner master either the *flat*

Figure 10-6. Backhand Ground Stroke.

or *slice* serve and leave the *American twist* serve for the more advanced player.

Flat or Cannon Ball Serve

This serve is hit with a flat racket face and places great speed on the ball. The ball is tossed slightly to the right of the shoulder holding the racket to a height above the full extension of the arm and racket.

Slice Serve

Spin is placed on the ball with this serve because of the ball and racket positioning. The ball is tossed more to the left of the shoulder over the right eye. The arm and racket are not fully extended as in the flat serve. The ball will curve toward the right side of the opponent's service court.

Grip. The slice serve is performed with an eastern grip. This type of grip will impart spin on the ball. To execute a flat or cannon ball serve, the western grip should be utilized.

Stance. Take a position when serving into the right service court approximately one foot to the right of the center mark and a few inches behind the baseline. When serving into the left service area, take a position to the left of the center line approximately 2 to 3 feet and a few inches behind the baseline. These positions will assure proper placement of the ball during the serve at your opponent's backhand. The racket is held at its throat in the left hand and the right elbow close to the body. The racket head is tilted up and points in the direction of the serve. The feet are comfortably placed with the weight evenly distributed and pointing in the direction of the serve.

Ball Toss. The ball is positioned in the air by an extension of the arm and hand, beginning at the wrist and ending in full extension forward of the right shoulder. Toss or boost the ball into the air with little or no spin, keeping the tossing hand fairly close to the body and moving upward with a motion which moves up in front of your face. Proper height for the toss may be determined by extending the arm and racket directly overhead. Toss the ball slightly higher than the racket head.

Backswing. From the service stance position the player drops his racket directly down in a circular motion. As the racket arm passes the rear leg the left hand begins to initiate the toss. The racket continues its upward motion to a position head high with the wrist in an uncocked position. At the head high position the elbow bends and the racket head comes up, dropping behind the back of the head and the racket is positioned behind the player's head, as if he were combing the back of his head with the racket. The trunk and shoulders have rotated away from the net. The weight is transferred to the rear foot and the back arches. At this time the ball has reached the peak of its height.

Contact With the Ball. The player lifts or reaches straight up with the racket from the back of the head combing position. The arm is fully extended and the ball is contacted at the peak or beginning of its descent. As the racket makes contact, the server snaps his wrist forward and down (like closing a window) to give the ball power and placement. The above movement is also similar to throwing a baseball directly overhead.

Follow Through. The racket arm continues its forward and downward movement and the racket swings freely down past the left side of the body. The body weight is now transferred to the right foot which crosses the baseline and continues forward taking a step in the direction of the serve to help maintain balance. The left foot is anchored to the court to insure body balance and an excellent follow through. (See Figure 10-7)

The Volley

The volley is used primarily when playing near the net to hit the ball before it bounces. The volley is also known as the "put away" shot. If it is executed properly the ball can be placed or *angled out* of the opponent's reach for a possible sure *winner*.

The Grip. The grip for the volley is identical to that employed in the execution of the forehand and backhand ground strokes.

Court position. The volley position is about six or eight feet from

Figure 10-7. The Serve.

the net. In singles, the net position is on the center service line midway between the net and service line. In the doubles game, the net position for either right or left service court is the same as in singles in relation to the net and service line, but midway between the center service line and the doubles side line.

Stance and Pivot. The ready position is assumed when executing the volley. The head of the racket is held slightly higher than in the forehand and backhand ground strokes. From the ready position, the player pivots as in the beginning of the forehand and backhand strokes. Footwork is essential in the proper execution of the volley. Keep in mind that a player should assume the side position when possible.

Backswing. There is little or no backswing in the volley. The wrist is cocked so that the head of the racket never drops below wrist level. The left hand is positioned on the throat of the racket until the racket begins its forward motion in preparation for contact with the ball.

Forward Swing. The racket arm comes toward the net and the ball in a downward and forward motion to meet the ball out in front of the body. The player's weight transfers from the back foot to the forward foot on contact. On contact with the ball, the wrist is locked and the elbow is close to the body. The volley stroke is a *poke, push,* or *punch* motion. The ideal volley would be made shoulder high. On a low shot the player bends down to the ball tilting the racket back. The lower the ball the more a player must open the racket face in order to send the ball over the net.

Follow Through. There is a slight follow through in the direction of the intended shot. Limit the extent of the follow through so that the poke, push, or punch motion is used and a very short follow through will result on completion of the volley return to the volley position.

Additional Strokes

The following explanation of strokes will complete the strokes to be learned and mastered if a player wishes to continue beyond the beginner's level of play and advance to a higher level of skill.

The Half Volley

This is a *pick up* shot made about midcourt by a player out of proper net position. The ball is hit immediately after it bounces with a stiff arm and wrist block and the body is bent well down toward the level of the ball. There is no backswing or follow through and the racket tilts slightly upward to direct the ball over the net.

The Lob

The grip, stance, footwork and backswing for the lob are similar to those used for the forehand and backhand ground strokes. The racket head tilts upward at contact with the ball and the racket arm continues slightly upward sending the ball high into the air. It is a high shot directed over the opponent's head deep into the backcourt. The lob can keep the net-rusher "honest" and many times provides valuable time for a player driven out of position by an opponent's shot.

The Overhead Smash

The smash is similar to the serve and all principles for executing the serve are generally applied to the overhead smash. The big difference is that the player must move and position himself directly under the descending ball. There is a slight pause after the racket has been driven back and the feet often leave the court on completion.

Singles Strategy

1. Warm-up properly. Practice all of your shots before starting the match.
2. Pay attention to your opponent's strengths and weaknesses during the warm-up period.
3. Keep the ball in play until the opportunity for placement arises.
4. Never change a winning game, but always change a losing game.
5. Against a net rusher, or highly skilled volleyer, use the passing shot, the angled cross-court and the lob.
6. Hit the ball deep to keep the opponent on the defensive.
7. Vary placement and pace of the ball.
8. Play just one point at a time.
9. Against a baseline player in singles, hit most shots cross court.
10. Play to the opponent's weakness, but don't overdo it.
11. Be alert to anticipate opponent's returns.
12. Bisect the angle of your opponent's possible return.

Doubles Strategy

1. Hit the ball deep to the center of the court.
2. The player with the strongest serve should always serve the first game for his team as each set begins.
3. Get the first serve in and advance to the net position.
4. Both doubles players play as parallel as possible—never one up and one back.
5. In good doubles play the most consistent return of service is the hard cross court forehand or backhand.
6. Singles depends on individual effort. Doubles requires good team work, by saying "mine" or "yours."
7. Play to the weakness of either or both opponents.
8. Cover partner's area when he is drawn out of court making a return.
9. Make use of the lob to drive your opponents from the net.
10. Hit the ball between your opponents or at their feet when you are at the net with them.

RULES

Court

The dimensions of the court for singles and doubles are as shown in Figure 10-2.

Server and Receiver

The "server" is the player who puts the ball into play and the "receiver" is his opponent.

Choice of Sides or Service

1. The winner of the toss has the choice of:
    a. Serving or receiving.
    b. Side of court.
2. The toss is made by placing the head of the racket on the court and spinning it. As it spins, the opponent calls some differentiating characteristic on the racket such as roughness or smoothness of the trim at the top and bottom of the racket head or a trademark.

Service Delivery

1. Before the server begins to serve, he must stand with both feet behind the base line within imaginary extensions of the center mark and side line.
2. The service always begins to the right of the center mark and is made to the opponent's right service court. After each point is played, service courts are changed for the next service in alternating fashion.
3. The server has two service attempts to put the ball into play.
4. The serve is made by tossing the ball into the air and hitting it with the racket before it touches the ground.
5. The ball must clear the net and land in the proper service court or on one of the lines of the proper service court before being hit by the receiver. However, after the service the ball may be hit before it bounces.

Foot Fault

1. During the delivery of the service, the server must not:
    a. Change his position by walking or running.
    b. Touch with either foot any area other than that behind the base line within imaginary extensions of the center mark and side line.

2. The rear foot may swing over the base line before the ball is struck if it does not touch the court.

Court Position For Service

1. In delivering the service, the server shall stand alternately behind the right and left courts, beginning from the right in every game. If service from a wrong half of the court occurs and is undetected, all play resulting from such wrong service or services shall stand, but the inaccuracy of the station shall be corrected immediately, when it is discovered.
2. The ball served shall pass over the net and hit the ground within the service court which is diagonally opposite, or upon any line bounding such court, before the receiver returns it. In the absence of a linesman and umpire, it is customary for the receiver to determine whether the service is good or not.

Faults

1. The service is a fault if the server:
   a. Does not take the proper position before serving.
   b. Commits a foot fault.
   c. Misses the ball in attempting to strike it. However, the server may toss and catch the ball without penalty.
   d. Fails to hit the ball into the proper service court.
   e. Serves the ball so that it hits a permanent structure other than the net, strap, or band.
   f. Hits his partner or anything he wears or carries with the served ball.
2. If any of these occurs on the first service, it is a single fault.
3. If any of these occurs on both services, it is a double fault and the point is lost.

Service After a Fault

After a fault (if it be the first fault), the server shall serve again from behind the same half of the court from which he served that fault, unless the service was from the wrong half, the server shall be entitled to one service only from behind the other half. A fault may not be claimed after the next service has been delivered.

The Let

1. A let is a ball which on service touches the net, strap, or band and is otherwise good.

2. A let is called when a player is unable to play a shot due to circumstances beyond his control such as interference by a ball or a player from another court.
3. A let also occurs if a service is delivered before the receiver is ready. If, however, the receiver attempts to return the service, he is considered to be ready.
4. When a let occurs on a service, only that service is repeated; if it occurs during play, the point is replayed (this allows two services).

Player Loses Point

A player loses the point if:
1. The ball bounces twice on his side of the net or if he does not return the ball to his opponent's court.
2. His body, clothing, or racket touch the net while the ball is in play.
3. He reaches over the net to play a ball unless the ball has bounced back over the net due to spin or to the wind.
4. The ball strikes him during play even if he is out-of-bounds.
5. He throws the racket at the ball and makes an otherwise good return.
6. He hits the ball more than once. In doubles the ball may be returned by only one partner.

Player Hinders Opponent

If a player commits any act either deliberate or involuntary which, in the opinion of the umpire, *hinders* his opponent in making a stroke, the umpire shall in the first case award the point to the opponent, and in the second case order the point to be replayed.

Good Returns

It is a good return if:
1. The ball lands on any boundary line.
2. The ball touches the top of a net post or the net and falls into the proper court.
3. A player goes beyond the net posts to play a ball and successfully returns it outside the posts and either above or below the net height.
4. A player follows through over the net but does not touch the net.

Scoring

1. The server's score is always called first.
2. The score in tennis is *15* for the first point won, *30* for the second, *40* for the third point, and the fourth point is *game*. A score of zero is referred to as *love*. When each side has a score of 40, the score is *deuce*, which means that one side must win two consecutive points in order to win the game. If the server wins the next point, the score is called *advantage in* and if he wins the following point it is game. If the receiver wins the first point after deuce, the score is called *advantage out* and if he wins the next point it is his *game*. However, if, after the score is either advantage in or advantage out, the other player wins the next point, the score then becomes deuce again.
3. The side reaching six games first wins the *set* unless the score is five games apiece, called a *deuce set*, in which case one side must gain a two-game lead in order to win the set. Two out of three sets constitutes a *match;* however, in some tournaments men play three out of five sets.

Changing Sides

The players change sides of court at the end of the first, third, and every subsequent alternate game of each set, and at the end of each set; unless the total number of games in such a set is even, in which case the change is not made until the end of the first game of the next set.

Serving In Doubles

The order of serving is decided at the beginning of each set. The pair serving first decides who is to serve in the first game, and the other partner will serve in the third game. The opponents also decide who is to serve first in the second game, and the other partner will serve in the fourth game. Both pairs alternate in the remaining games of the set.

The server's partner may stand anywhere during the service, but he usually stands within eight feet of the net and in a position so that he can cover his half of the court.

If a player serves out of turn, the proper server must serve as soon as the mistake is discovered. All points earned are counted. If a complete game is played with the wrong server, the order of service remains as altered.

Receiving In Doubles

The order of receiving is decided at the beginning of each set. The pair receiving in the first game decides who will receive first, and that player will continue to receive first in all odd numbered games of the set. The opponents will also decide who will receive first in the second game, and he will receive the first service in all even numbered games of the set. Players alternate receiving services during a game.

TERMINOLOGY

Ace—Good service that is not touched by the opponent.

Ad—Abbreviation for advantage.

Advantage—Next point after deuce. "Advantage in" refers to the server's winning the point, and "advantage out" refers to the receiver's winning the point.

All—Tie score. This is used when deuce is not applicable, such as "30 all."

Alley—Area between the singles side line and the side line on a doubles court.

Backcourt—Area of the court between the service line and the base line. This area is commonly known as "No Man's Land."

Backhand—Stroke used to hit balls on the left side of a right-handed player and on the right side of a left-handed player.

Backspin—Rotation of the ball so that the top of the ball spins backward.

Base Line—Line at each end of the court.

Break a Serve—Phrase used to indicate winning a game that the opponent served.

Center Mark—Mark four inches long and two inches wide that bisects the base line to indicate one limit of the proper service area.

Center Service Line—Line down the center of the court that separates the service courts.

Center Strap—Two-inch-wide piece of canvas that holds the net down at the center.

Chop—Stroke in which the racket is drawn sharply down under the ball to give it backspin.

Cross-Court—Phrase indicating a ball hit diagonally from one corner across the net to another corner.

Deuce—Even score when each side has won three or more points.

Double Fault—Failure on two consecutive services.

Doubles—Play with two persons on each side.

Drive—Shot hit hard without much of an arc so that it lands near the opponent's base line.

Error—Failure to make a legal return when racket has hit the ball.

Fault—Failure to make a legal service.

Foot Fault—Illegal movement of the feet during service.

Forecourt—Area of the court between the net and the service line.

Forehand—Stroke used to hit balls on the right side of a right-handed player and on the left side of a left-handed player.

Game—Unit of a set completed by winning four points before opponent wins three, or by winning two consecutive points after deuce.

Ground Stroke—Stroke made by hitting the ball after it has bounced.

Half-Volley—Stroke made by hitting the ball immediately after it has hit the ground.

Kill—Hard-hit or well-placed ball that the opponent cannot reach for a return.

Let—Service or point that is to be replayed because of some type of interference.

Lob—Shot hit with a high arc so that it lands near the opponent's base line.

Love—Zero score.

Match—Contest between two or four players, usually consisting of two out of three sets.

Match Point—Point that, if won, allows a player to win the match.

Overhead Smash—Shot made with a hard overhead stroke so that the ball comes down sharply into the opponent's court. This shot is usually referred to as the "smash."

Pass—Shot going to either side of an opponent near the net out of his reach.

Rally—Continued play between the serve and the winning of a point.

Service—Putting the ball into play.

Set—Unit of a match completed by winning six games, or by winning two consecutive games after each team has won five games.

Set Point—Point that, if won, allows a player to win the set.

Singles—Play with one person on each side of the net.

Slice—Stroke in which the racket is drawn sharply down across the ball with wrist action to give sidespin.

Topspin—Rotation of the ball so that the top of the ball spins forward.

Toss—The spin of the racket at the beginning of a match to determine choice of serving or receiving, or side of court.

Trim—Small stringing at top and bottom of racket head to hold the main strings in place. This stringing is used in the toss to indicate "rough" or "smooth." The rough side contains the loops around the main strings while the smooth is the opposite side.

Volley—Ball hit in the air before it bounces.

BIBLIOGRAPHY

Barnaby, John M. *Racket Work: the Key to Tennis.* Boston: Allyn and Bacon, Inc., 1969.

Everett, Peter, Dumas, Virginia. *Beginning Tennis.* California: Wadsworth Publishing Company, 1962.

Johnson, Joan D., Xanthos, Paul J. *Tennis.* Iowa: Wm. C. Brown Company Publishers, 1967.

Kenfield, John F., Jr. *Teaching and Coaching Tennis.* Dubuque, Iowa: Wm. C. Brown Company Publishers, 1964.

Pelton, Barry C. *Tennis.* California: Goodyear Publishing Company, Inc., 1969.

CHAPTER

11

VOLLEYBALL

BEHAVIORAL OBJECTIVES

1. Under simulated game conditions, given a volleyball, the college student will be able to successfully demonstrate (meet all of the essential criteria as specified in the chapter) the following volleyball skills:
   a. Ready position.
   b. Underhand serve.
   c. Overhand serve.
   d. Overhead pass.
   e. Set-up.
   f. Underhand Bump pass.
   g. Dig.
   h. Spike.
   i. Block.
2. The college student will be able to achieve a score of at least 75 per cent on a written examination concerned with the history, rules, strategy, terminology and analysis of volleyball fundamentals.

HISTORY OF VOLLEYBALL

Volleyball was developed in 1895 by William J. Morgan, who at that time was physical education director of the Y.M.C.A. in Holyoke, Massachusetts. His reason for inventing this game was to provide an indoor game for the winter months in which relatively large groups of men could participate in a small gymnasium. Mr. Morgan employed the principal features of tennis, but the net was raised and the players struck the ball with their hands instead of rackets.

The Y.M.C.A. is chiefly credited with promoting this very fine game to prominence. It soon spread to the Orient and South

America. It spread widely in America, and today it is played regularly on playgrounds, in recreation centers, camps, school gymnasium classes, and school and college intramural leagues. It is one of the best of the after-school carry-over team sports.

The Y.M.C.A. held its first National Volleyball Championships in 1922. Since that time, this has been an annual tournament for Y.M.C.A. teams and has done much to further popularize the game.

NATURE OF VOLLEYBALL

Volleyball for men is played on a court 60 feet by 30 feet, divided into two halves, with a net eight feet high, with two teams of six players each. In women's play, the net is only seven feet four and one-quarter inches high. The six players are designated as left, center, and right forwards and left, center, and right backs—or they may be numbered from one to six, starting with the left forward. When it is a team's turn to serve, every player rotates one position clockwise and the right back serves.

The object of the game is to keep the ball from striking the floor on your side of the net and to return it so that it strikes the floor on your opponents' side so they cannot return it. The ball is put in play from behind the rear boundary line by the right back, who serves it across the net into the opponents' court. The ball is then volleyed back and forth until one team or the other fails to return the ball. If the serving team makes the error, it loses the serve. An error by the receiving team gives one point to the servers. A team can score only when it serves, and it continues to serve as long as it scores. A ball may be volleyed twice before being played over the net, which makes a total of three hits per side, except, of course, that the serve must go directly from the server to the opponents' court. A match consists of two out of three games. Sides are changed after the first and second games and at the middle (eight points or four minutes for women) of the third game.

EQUIPMENT

Ball

Most volleyballs are made of either leather sections or of a solid, rubberized material. The ball must measure between 25 and 27 inches in circumference with a weight of nine to ten ounces. In addition, the balls should be inflated to a pressure between 7 and 8 pounds.

Net

A volleyball net measures 32 feet long by 3 feet wide. The netting is made up of four-inch-square mesh. When installed, the net should measure 8 feet above the playing surface in the center. The net should be stretched tightly across the court so that balls hitting it will rebound properly.

Standards

Standards, or *uprights*, hold the net with the use of a tightly drawn cable. These standards should be at least three feet outside the sideline of the court.

SKILLS TO BE DEVELOPED

Body Position

The first skill a player should learn in order to play the ball correctly is body position. This means the player's hands are up to receive the ball, his weight is evenly distributed, and his body is slightly crouched to spring into action. One foot is usually slightly ahead of the other, and both eyes follow the flight of the ball. As the ball is hit, the player should be moving in anticipation of receiving it. After he gains experience, he learns to recognize signs that indicate where the ball will probably go. The position of the ball before it is hit and the position of his team's defense are two of the common signs. The first step seems to be the hardest one since it initiates body action. Ideally, it should be toward the ball. (See Figure 11-1)

Figure 11-1. Getting Ready to Play the Ball.

Serving

Although there are many kinds of serves, there are only two basic methods of putting the ball in play—the other serves being, for the most part, variations of the overhand and underhand serves.

Underhand Serve. This is the simplest, easiest, and safest way to start play. To make an underhand serve, stand facing the net with the ball resting in the left hand. Move the right arm back below shoulder height and then swing it straight forward, knocking the ball off the left hand with the palm and heel of the right hand. It is necessary to follow through by straightening the left knee at the moment of contact and by letting the right hand follow the path of the ball. An effective "floater" can be hit if the ball is moved backward, then forward, with the left hand as the right hand follows and strikes the ball without spinning it. The ball may also be struck with the palm side of the closed fist or with the thumb and forefinger of a semiclosed fist. (See Figure 11-2)

a.   b.

Figure 11-2. Underhand Serve.

Overhand Serve. This is an advanced serve to be learned only after the underhand serve has been thoroughly mastered. To perform the overhand serve, stand facing the net with the left foot advanced, and the ball resting in the left hand or on both hands in front of the body. Toss the ball from three to five feet above the head. Raise the right hand up and back with the upper arm parallel to the ground, and arch the back with the hips forward. As the ball falls, cup the hand and hit it with the heel, palm and fingers just above the height of the head. Follow through by letting the hand follow the ball flight, straightening the right leg and turning the body from right to left. The entire movement is quite similar to making an overhand baseball throw. The idea is to hit a hard floater that is difficult to return due to the downward trajectory of the service. (See Figure 11-3)

Placement of the Serve. Every serve should be made so it necessitates either a long pass to the set-up man or a pass moving in the same direction as that in which the set-up man will have to pass to

a.   b.   c.

Figure 11-3. Overhand Serve.

his attack partner. This means that all serves should be made to the extreme back corners of the receiving court.

If the set-up player is in the center forward position, the best serve is to the right back, and if the set-up player is in the right forward position, the best serve is to the left back.

Passing

Overhead Pass. In order to execute an effective overhead pass, the receiver must get in position under the ball. The arms, wrist and fingers play a dominant role in the overhead pass. The elbows should be above shoulder height with the wrists extended as far back as possible. The elbows are out and the fingers are slightly cupped, so that the ball is contacted by all the fingers and thumbs at the same time. The ball must be played on the pads of the fingers and thumbs, not the fingertips or palms. The index fingers and thumbs should point in at each other so that a triangle is formed. The hands are about six inches apart with the fingers spread fairly wide. (See Figure 11-4) Upon contact, the elbows are extended, sending the ball in a high arc without spin to the set man.

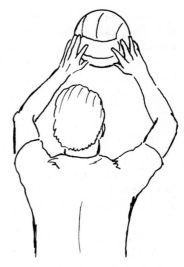

Figure 11-4. Position of Hands for Overhand Pass.

Underhand Bump Pass. All balls that cannot be received with an overhand pass should be bounced upward using an underhand pass. The purpose of the underhand pass or *bump pass* is to keep the ball in play. After a great deal of practice, the bump pass can become very accurate and can be used to set up a spiker. In order to execute the bump pass, place the fingers of one hand on the fingers of the other, palms up. Next, place the thumbs on the index finger of the top hand. (See Figure 11-5) Hold your arms as close together as possible with the elbows together and rotated inward. The result of these movements should be a broad, flat surface running from your elbows to your thumbs.

To assume the proper body position for the bump pass, the knees are bent into a crouching position with one foot slightly ahead of the other. It is important to keep the arms away from the body and to play the ball off the flat extended surface of the forearms. (See Figure 11-6) Balls hitting off the fingers or thumbs are difficult to control. As the ball is contacted, the knees straighten with the arms moving in a parallel manner from the floor up. If the ball is over the head, then the whole body must turn and the ball must be played over the shoulder using a backwards bump pass. It is important to remember that only in the backwards bump pass are the elbows flexed in order to return the ball over the shoulder in the opposite direction.

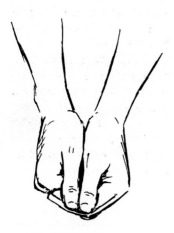

Figure 11-5. Position of
Hands for Bump Pass.

Figure 11-6. Body Position
for Bump Pass.

Dig. Balls that are hit just outside of a player's normal reach can be received by using a one-hand bump pass. Such a maneuver is called a *dig.* The dig is per-formed by extending the arm at the side of the body to which the ball is hit. The knees are slightly bent with the body weight forward on the balls of the feet. Upon contact, the knees are straight-ened as the player attempts to strike the ball on the forearm or wrist with the arm moving in an upward direction. (See Figure 11-7)

Figure 11-7. Dig.

Setting-Up

In order to provide a favorable opportunity for the spike, the ball must be set-up. By passing the ball high above and close to the net, the set-up thus makes possible an effective execution of the spike. The set-up is actually an application of the overhead pass. The key to a good set is getting into position quickly. The most desired position is one in which the ball is coming down in front of the setter's face and the setter is facing the man to whom he is going to set up. As in the overhead pass, the index fingers and thumbs are pointing in toward each other with the elbows out to the sides. Fingers should be slightly flexed and spread about an inch apart at the tips. For the most part, only the thumbs, forefingers and index fingers make con-tact with the ball. As the ball comes into the hands, it is received on the fingertips; the fingers and wrists come back slightly with the ball as the arms absorb the initial shock of the ball. The ball is then flicked out with an outward and upward extension of the arms. The set-up should be hit upward toward the ceiling, not directly at a teammate. There should be no spin on the ball, and the set should be about ten feet above the net and in front of the intended spiker.

Spiking

Spiking is the term used for hitting a ball that is above and close to the net downward into the opponents' court. This type of delivery is very difficult to return and is the specialty of a winning team. The spiker should hit the ball near its top. The ball must be higher than the net when it is hit; hence the spiker must jump up to make the hit.

As the jump is made, the hand is brought up above the head behind the shoulder; the wrist is superextended (cocked) with the palm facing the net (See Figure 11-8) The spiker handles the ball with the tips of his fingers, flexing the wrist violently at the time of contact with the ball to force the ball downward into the front area of the opponents' court. (See Figure 11-9)

Figure 11-8. Cocking Position for Arm in Spike.

Figure 11-9. Hitting Position for Arm in Spike.

Some good spikers hit with the heel of the hand and a closed fist. This makes a harder spike but one which is more difficult to control.

Contact with the ball is made with the heel of the hand with the fingers held rigidly. As the ball is hit, the hand is brought over on top of the ball to impart top spin so that it will curve down sharply to land in the opponents' court. (See Figure 11-10)

Blocking

Blocking is the technique employed by one or more defensive players to counteract the advantage gained by a good spike on the part of the offensive team. Essentially, it is the act of jumping with arms extended straight up and fingers tensed from a position directly in front of the ball at the time it is hit, and returning the ball

Figure 11-10. Body Position at
Contact of Spike.

immediately down into the opponents' court. The spring from the
floor is made from both feet with all blockers jumping in unison. The
spring should be made at sufficient distance from the net to permit
the arms to move forward at the moment of contact with the ball
without the danger of touching the net. When one wants to return
the ball to the opponents' court from the block, his fingers are held
vertical and the hands stiff. If he wants to merely retain control of it,
the hands and fingers are tensed but tilted backward. Timing is the
key to successful blocking. There is a tendency for inexperienced
players to jump too soon. One should be aware that he must delay
his jump until the last possible moment. The more advanced the
play, the larger the number of blockers that are used. Beginners use
one or possibly two, while advanced team play calls for three or four
blockers. International rules permit only two blockers.

Playing Strategy

1. Play to the opponents' weaknesses, such as a weak man and the
   poorest defensive man at the net.
2. Usually serve to your opponents' back right court unless there is
   a left-handed spiker up. When opponents' spiker is in the center-
   forward position, it is best to serve to your opponents' back left
   court.

3. Study the defensive tactics of your opponents and play to their weaknesses.
4. Serve quickly when you are piling up points.
5. Study each spiker and set your defenses to stop his placements.
6. The spiker should not hit the ball straight down the center unless the center forward fails to block.

Playing Courtesies

Volleyball is an unusually sportsmanlike team game. This is true probably because the players are on opposite sides of the net, and there is very little occasion for bodily contact with opponents. If one wishes to be a good sport in volleyball, he should observe the following courtesies:

1. Always return the ball on the floor to the next server.
2. In case of doubt, call the play in favor of the opponents.
3. Compliment the opponents for a good play.
4. Call own fouls, quickly and honestly.

Safety

The possibility of accidental injury to a player in volleyball is less than in sports in which there is a great deal of bodily contact. However, it is important that every player stay in his assigned position to avoid collision with a teammate; in their eagerness to play the ball, players often forget this safety precaution. Often a number of finger injuries are incurred during a game. These can be prevented by acquiring the skills of correct ball handling and by special exercises to increase the strength of the fingers.

Helpful Points

Volleyball is a great team game that requires more skill and provides an opportunity for more organized effort than is generally thought.

The following hints may help one to become a skilled player:

1. Learn to control the underhand serve so that you can place it "on a dime."
2. Master the skill of receiving a ball on the finger tips but "with the whole body" so that it can be passed or set up as light as a feather.
3. Spike with the hand relaxed so the fingers wrap around the ball.

4. Play the ball underhand with the bump pass.
5. Usually set the ball in the center of the net—this allows the spiker to hit in any direction.
6. To play ball out of the net, squat low and play it straight up.

RULES OF VOLLEYBALL

1. A ball may be played off the net except on the service.
2. The ball must always pass over the net within the side boundaries.
3. A ball hitting the net and going over is good except on the service.
4. Players may change positions at the start of the game but not during the game.
5. The losing team serves first in the second game. The opponents then rotate for their first serve.

Fouls and Violations

1. Stepping on or over the line while serving the ball results in loss of serve.
2. Stepping over the line under the net. Stepping on the line is permitted.
3. Reaching over the net (except during follow-through of spike).
4. Touching the net with any part of the body while the ball is in play.
5. Playing the ball twice in succession, or allowing it to hit two places on the body during the same play.
6. Lifting, scooping, shoving, following, or allowing the ball to come to rest momentarily in the hands.
7. Allowing the ball to touch the clothing or the body below the hips.
8. Four hits.
9. Serving out of turn. The serve is lost, and no points made by the server count.
10. Reaching under the net and playing the ball while the opponents are playing it.
11. Any double foul, that is, each side fouling on the same play, makes the ball dead.

TERMINOLOGY

Actual playing time—The time between contact on the serve and a dead ball.

Add out—The team which has scored one point following a tie after any score from 14 on.

Block—Defensive play by players (or a player) in the forward positions who place their hands and arms above the net so that a spiked ball rebounds into the opponents' court or back to their own.

Bump pass—The forearm bounce pass made on low balls.

Catching or holding the ball—The ball must be clearly batted. If it rests momentarily in a player's hands, it is considered illegal.

Dead ball—The ball is dead following a point, sideout, or any decision temporarily suspending the play.

Delaying the game—Any player who, in the opinion of the referee, is unnecessarily slowing down the game.

Deuce—When the score is tied at any point from 14 on.

Dig pass—A pass made with the hand slightly cupped or with the fist of one hand, usually on a difficult play.

Double foul—Infraction of rules by both teams during the same play.

Dribbling—When a player touches a ball more than once in succession.

Game point—The last point in a game.

Out of bounds—When a ball touches outside a boundary line. If it touches a boundary line it is good.

Playing the ball—Any player who is in the act of touching the ball.

Point—A point is scored when the receiving team fails to return the ball legally to the opponents' court.

Rotation—Shifting of the players, clockwise, just before a "new" person serves.

Service—The right back puts the ball in play by batting it over the net to the opponents. His feet must be behind the rear service line.

Side out—Side is out when the serving team fails to win a point or plays the ball illegally.

BIBLIOGRAPHY

Armbruster, Irwin, and Musker. *Basic Skills in Sports for Men and Women.* Saint Louis: C.V. Mosby Company, 1967.

Fait, Shaw, and Ley. *A Manual of Physical Education Activities.* Philadelphia: W.B. Saunders Company, 1969.

Hartman, Paul E. *Volleyball.* Columbus, Ohio: Charles E. Merrill Publishing Company, 1968.

Means, and Jack. *Physical Education Activities, Sports and Games.* Dubuque: Wm. C. Brown Company Publishers, 1968.

Seaton, Clayton, Leibee, and Messersmith. *Physical Education Handbook.* Englewood Cliffs: Prentice-Hall, Inc., 1969.